"Janet Etty-Leal is one of Australia's most experienced and passionate mindfulness educators and it is exciting to see her work come to life in this resource developed specifically for Early Learning educators. 'A Head-Heart Start for Life: Creative Mindful Discoveries for Young Children' provides a structured guide for educators to introduce creative and engaging mindful activities in to their classrooms to help young minds develop essential life skills to grow and flourish."
– HAYLEY ANTHONY Educational Psychologist and lecturer, Monash University

"Janet has been cultivating the art and science of teaching children mindfulness for over 20 years. In her latest book, 'A Head-Heart Start for Life', Janet brings to life mindful wisdom for young children. The clearly and artfully written lesson plans will help teachers nourish skills such as curiosity, creativity, kindness and compassion in the classroom. I highly recommend teachers and schools purchase a copy of Janet's text and embark on a path of mindful discovery."
– DR. NICOLE J ALBRECHT Course Co-ordinator – MindBody Wellness/Wellness & Health Assessment, RMIT University, Melbourne, Australia

"Janet has worked with my staff and students over a period of 13 years. Her approach has become part of the school culture and her input has been invaluable to our school community.

This book is a must have for teachers and schools wanting to develop a holistic approach to health and wellbeing for children. Each lesson is structured with clear learning intentions, which take the guess work out of planning and implementation for teachers. It is easy to understand and fun to follow for children."
– BILL LISTON Principal, Yarraman Oaks Primary School

"Janet Etty-Leal has written an important book to assist teachers, parents and carers. She has integrated stories, strategies, and daily routines to help children build focus and connection – to themselves and their communities. There are many practical and inspirational ideas inside that will help children."
– TOM BRUNZELL Senior Advisor Education, Berry Street Childhood Institute

"Here is a remarkable book that offers a host of practical and user-friendly techniques which parents and teachers can use to stimulate children's imagination through relaxation and attentional training. The beguilingly simple strategies will also enable children to directly access feelings of awe and wonderment."
– BOB SHARPLES Psychologist

A Head-Heart

Start for Life

Creative Mindful Discoveries for Young Children

JANET ETTY-LEAL

Illustrations by Lee Lai

meditation
capsules

First published in Australia in 2018 by
Meditation Capsules
PO Box 17
Kew East
VIC 3102
Telephone: +61 (0) 408 531 618
Email: janet@meditationcapsules.com
www.meditationcapsules.com

Editorial contributions by Aimee Bloom and Diane Berold
Cover and text designed by R. T. J. Klinkhamer
Cover and text illustrations by Lee Lai
Printed in Australia by Focus Print Group, Melbourne

A cataloguing-in-publication entry is available from the catalogue of the
National Library of Australia at www.nla.gov.au.

Contents

PROGRAM

In loving memory of my parents,
Barbara and Wally,
who provided a magical childhood.

Foreword

As someone who, for the last decade, has been directly involved in helping schools and educators around the world to embed wellbeing into school systems, I have come across my fair share of 'experts' who, though well-intentioned, lack a genuine understanding of what lies at the heart of great teaching. I often meet someone new in the wellbeing field and find myself wondering if this new person would really be able to 'know' or to 'see' my two-year old son – would they really know what it takes to inspire him, to grow his engagement with the world, to help him love learning.

I have always been a bit of an 'optimistic sceptic'. New educational concepts, ideas and possibilities excite me, but it takes some convincing for me to 'buy-in'. This was certainly the case with Mindfulness. So, when I first heard about Janet Etty-Leal's work and then had the chance to meet her in 2013, I was interested but cautious. In my then role as Head of Positive Education at Geelong Grammar School, I was aware that she had been working with students for a number of years. I had also read her first book, 'Meditation Capsules', which many Australian teachers were using in classrooms, but until that stage I was unsure if Mindfulness could really be 'taught' effectively to students in a classroom context. *Was there really anything special about Janet's approach to exploring Mindfulness with students? Was there anything different about her style or her teaching or her philosophy that was worth sharing?*

What I probably didn't really understand about Mindfulness was that it is a way of living – 'a life skill' as Janet puts it. And what I didn't know about Janet at the time was that this was a person who walks her talk! I vividly remember my first meeting with Janet and, in a quite beautiful way, feeling almost unsettled by her present-centeredness. It felt so clear to me that everything I said really mattered – because in that moment – our conversation was all that mattered to her. Even today, now having known and worked with Janet for years, whenever I meet with her, I'm aware of an unusual sense of connection when we speak and when I see her speak with others – educators and students.

I'm sure part of this ability comes from her years of practising and teaching Mindfulness. However, in addition to this layer of experience,

Janet is a great teacher and it is this foundation that makes her work so impactful, relevant and inspiring. Having spent more than 35 years in the classroom, Janet is an inspiring teacher first, but also a deeply passionate Mindfulness expert who *really* understands children and how to teach Mindfulness differently – in a way that makes so much sense to young minds.

Janet's mission is to bring her insight, experience and creative methodology to others by sharing practical activities and implementable strategies. She understands how busy and stretched teachers are and knows that what we really need are simple, clear, reliable, creative, novel materials, instructions and strategies that we can use immediately with our students. And it's hard to imagine a person better placed than Janet to write a book full of ready-to-go material for Early Learning Centre (ELC) teachers.

Yet, Janet has managed to stay true to her core belief that teaching Mindfulness is easy – but teaching Mindfulness *well* requires a teacher to thoughtfully draw on their creativity and fundamental understanding of a child's experience *and* requires an authentic personal experience with Mindfulness practice.

In this book, Janet has continued to both incorporate the latest scientific understanding of the behavioural and neurosciences and to challenge traditional 'textbook' thinking about teaching Mindfulness in schools. So many educators I come across are eager to incorporate Mindfulness into their teaching but don't quite know where to start or how to do it well.

Janet's work fills this gap. Whether it's speaking at national and international conferences, serving on boards, consulting with school leaders, or in her work directly with teachers and students, Janet is so committed to generously sharing her passion and experience with us all.

So, I'm really excited for you the reader, the passionate ELC educator, to get your hands on this book. You are already a wonderful, committed, passionate teacher – you wouldn't be reading this if you weren't. And you're about to be inspired even further.

David Bott
Associate Director
Institute of Positive Education
Geelong Grammar School
Author, *Teach Positive*

Preface

My journey of sharing the skills of Mindfulness and Meditation with children began at home 20 years ago. Spontaneous Mindful opportunities and intimate moments with my young daughters started the ball rolling. Our favourite times were pre-sleep. Lying together in bed, hands would become stars, softly ascending with each gentle outbreath to find a soothing landing place on the tummy or heart.

My girls loved these practices. They developed both a sense of awareness of the gifts at their fingertips and the agency to discover their own personal ways to feel centred and calm.

As I introduced programs in schools in Years 11 and 12, I realised these needed to start in Year 10, Year 8, Year 7, and ultimately in primary schools. Then, as my work in primary schools grew, I was invited to work in Early Learning Centres (ELCs). The more time I spent practising Mindfulness with little children, the more I became convinced about the need to develop Mindfulness skills with children in the Early Years.

Mindfulness offers a rich palette of possibilities for children to make their own discoveries. As the poet Mark Van Doren observed, *"The art of teaching is the art of assisting discovery"*. The brain loves novelty … and so do young children. All kinds of resources, concepts and activities can be used in a Mindfulness program. There are countless ways to fully engage children, light up neuronal connections and build positive neural networks.

Studies investigating the effects of preschool on educational outcomes remind us that Early Learning is a crucial time for development. Dr. Stacey Fox, a Mitchell Institute policy fellow at Victoria University, argues for two years of preschool education: *"Early education is at least as important as school"*. A study conducted by Melbourne University in 2013 showed that taking part in preschool and being taught by a qualified educator made a significant difference. Positive outcomes in reading and numeracy were clearly evident in Year 3.

Early Learning is a golden opportunity to develop the essential building blocks of not only numeracy and literacy, but also vital social concepts like communicating, co-operating and nurturing relationships.

Mindfulness brings rich opportunities that contribute much more to this foundation. Engaging in Mindful experiences harnesses children's innate ability to be present and curious, with boundless opportunities to nurture social and emotional learning. Young children have an insatiable delight for exploring the outer world and find playful, engaging experiences irresistible. Mindfulness helps to amplify and extend this beam of focus.

Practices can be simple and dovetail effortlessly into ELC programs, therapeutic modalities and in the home. Hours have been spent in my classes having great fun exploring what 'shape' the body is in. Enjoying all kinds of shapes that our feet and legs, hands and arms, torso and head can create. Noticing all kinds of ways in which the body can move, and how different shapes and movements on the outside can change our state of being on the inside.

The Mindful beam of focus can illuminate what is happening inside the body, creating an awareness of a whole inner world. Working with this age group offers a vital opportunity to engage children in noticing *without judging* – to notice with an open mind, with wonder and curiosity. This creates a precious foundation for life. Thus, the vital life skill of nurturing awareness with kindness and care is engendered, creating a wholesome, healthy relationship with the self.

Somatic-based inquiry activities create the perfect segue to learn more about the body and the magnificent, interconnected orchestra of parts that serve us. Psychiatrist and researcher Dr. Norman Doidge reminds us that 'the brain's way of healing is via the body'. Children can discover this themselves, through creative, playful practices; noticing the messages travelling to the brain from their feet and legs, hands and arms, tummy, lungs and heart. Children learn that they can choose where to direct their attention and literally make up their own minds, developing a growing sense of agency in taking care of their beautiful bodies and minds.

Character strengths can be seamlessly introduced into the program to help children identify special qualities and virtues that they possess. Recognising these strengths builds positive habits that are reflected in virtuous feelings, thoughts and actions.

A Mindfulness Program for young children can begin with baby steps, simply by cultivating opportunities to pause and notice. Mindful rituals can become part of the day, with opportunities for playful 'Mindful Punctuation' to bookend the day with greetings and farewells, create transitions between activities, or finding moments to refresh attention and awareness. Mindful rituals enhance a gentle sense of pattern and rhythm throughout the day.

In time, pauses and short practices can be gradually extended to create longer Meditation practices. Children can begin to discover the pleasure of taking time, slowing down and creating quiet spaces – to shift from doing to being, from thinking to sensing and feeling, and from busyness to stillness. Simple rituals before and after the practices instil a sense of how special such practices are. Mindfulness practices make the most of children's precious inner gifts and help them befriend and value themselves – to develop respect, to bond as a group and to nurture caring, connected relationships.

When children experience being quiet and still in a group, they magically discover how their shared, focused, quiet attention creates the sense of a sacred atmosphere. I never cease to feel deeply privileged and moved when sharing these moments with children.

By making simple investments to establish Mindfulness practices in ELCs and in the home, we can bring about positive outcomes and great rewards, supporting happy, focused children, harmonious communities and truly providing a head-heart start for life.

Janet Etty-Leal
January, 2018

Author's acknowledgements

As I write this, lyrics from the Beatles song 'With a little help from my friends' come to mind.

So many people have provided invaluable encouragement and support.

Thanks to Richard Rice, Managing Director of ELC One Early Education Group P/L, this book shifted from a long- cherished dream to a reality. Production was fast tracked by his commission for a Mindfulness Manual for his Cranbourne ELC Centre in February 2017. Mindfulness is practised daily at this Centre.

Author Tracy Chevalier observed that writing a book was like slowly transforming boulders into rocks, rocks into pebbles and pebbles into gem stones. Many wonderful minds have contributed to a long, careful process of refining and polishing this book.

Support has come in all kinds of ways. My friends Elissa Johnston and Bruce Dempsey graciously invited me to stay in their garden cottage in Port Fairy, which was a 'writing haven' to complete the book (in the Zen company of Arlo the rabbit).

Grateful thanks to Catherine Shepard, Still Point Yoga and Shakti Burke, Mindfulness in Education, Northern Rivers, for sharing their beautiful practices.

A long line of friends and colleagues reviewed countless drafts. Outstanding early learning educators, including Sonia Shard from CPS Child and Family Centre started this process.

It has been a blessing to work for over a decade with truly exceptional colleagues at Geelong Grammar School. The school enables me to work with creative, dedicated staff at three campuses who embrace my lessons with students and extend themes into the class curriculum and environment, with all kinds of installations, activities and projects. Brigette Vallance and Suzie Reeves offered valuable suggestions and insights to develop the program. Aimee Bloom shared her expertise to provide initial edits and recommendations. For many years, it was inspirational to work alongside Pam Barton, a gifted, passionate primary teacher at Geelong Grammar School, who has generously contributed to fine-tuning the manuscript. I greatly appreciate working with dedicated, passionate colleagues like

David Bott, Justin Robinson and Rhiannon McGee from the Positive Education Department and Training Institute at the school. And for well over a decade, it has been wonderful to have deep, meaningful discussions with John Hendry and Charlie Scudamore.

For over 15 years, Bob Sharples has literally been on call to support me with every step of my Mindful pathway! I am deeply grateful for his wisdom, support and guidance.

It is an absolute blessing to have friends like Pam Richards and Megan Jones, who are always available to share wisdom and support (and also helped fine-tune the book). Final polishing of the manuscript was expertly provided by Diane Berold. Her masterful editing transformed the text.

I am also blessed to have the incredible support of my brother, Matthew, who patiently deals with all my business issues and invested hours into proof reading. My partner Peter provides endless moral support, along with practical help making props and speaking sticks. And my beautiful daughters share their respective skills and gifts. With her legal expertise, Francesca is always available to guide me through business challenges. For over 15 years, Lee's drawings have provided creative, unique presentation slides and graphics for my work. I am thrilled to have her beautiful painting feature on the cover and her drawings grace the pages in this book.

Finally, it is a privilege and a joy to share practices with young children – my little teachers.

Introduction for teachers

"Every life is a piece of art, put together with all means available" — PIERRE JANET

Day by day, moment by moment, experiences are woven into the fabric of our lives. It is my pleasure to offer creative ideas, activities and Mindful practices to weave into the lives of young children to support their wellbeing and personal growth.

This program was designed and written to support you, as Early Learning educators, therapists and parents, to bring Mindfulness to life for children from three to six years of age.

Mindfulness is a life skill and a natural ability we all have – to be fully aware and engaged in life. The ability to sustain attention is a prerequisite of learning, accomplishment and relationships. This program cultivates this ability with curiosity and kindness.

A rich palette of inquiry-based, playful activities and approaches is designed to engage each child with opportunities to fully participate in each session and most importantly, to make meaningful and personal discoveries.

Years of research and countless hours spent working with young children have been invested to develop this program. It has been written to support the implementation of Mindfulness in Early Learning Centres, providing comprehensive guidelines and resources. Concepts and practices can also support therapeutic practice and family life.

The program provides you with structure for sessions, guidance for practices and suggestions for concepts and themes. However, it is important for you to realise that there is scope and flexibility for you to deliver the practices and sessions in a way that best suits your students, curriculum and circumstances. Use it with an open mind-set. Take every opportunity to use appropriate words, metaphors, stories, visual aids and props. Whenever possible, bring

Mindfulness to life for the children – connecting it to the seasons, awareness of nature, special events, celebrations and excursions. By doing so, we can help children realise that Mindfulness is a practice for life.

Positive Mindful outcomes for children and educators

A growing body of international research indicates that Mindfulness supports:

- Effective emotional regulation and stress management
- Opportunities for personal growth and happiness
- The creation of harmonious, creative and cooperative learning environments
- Effective integration into the curriculum and into life

Positive outcomes of Mindfulness practices can include:

- Improved focus and concentration
- Developing emotional literacy and behaviour management skills
- Enhanced resilience and self-efficacy
- Increased levels of optimism and empathy for others and the world
- Greater happiness and wellbeing

Mindfulness is a way of being. It involves cultivating compassion and developing a wise awareness of the self and others. The very best approach is to bring Mindfulness to life. Practices are to be 'lived', becoming part of the fabric of the day – not confined to one-off sessions timetabled during the week. You can enjoy becoming more Mindful yourself, developing a calm, 'heartful' approach to your work and to each child. You will find you are gradually replacing unconscious, rushed, reactive habits with conscious, kind responses and actions. Your *Mindful way of being* will become a powerful teaching model and a rewarding source of connection with children.

Simple, fun suggestions for 'Mindful Punctuations' are shared – little rituals for greetings, transitions and 'reset, refresh and retune' moments throughout the day.

Content of 'A Head-Heart Start for Life'

Findings from current neuroscience research underpin content of the program. Dr. Rick Hanson, author of 'Hardwiring Happiness: The New Brain Science of Contentment, Calm and Confidence', identifies three universal core needs – Safety, Satisfaction and Connection. The activities here address these needs. As children immerse themselves in sensory, play-based experiences, satisfying, happy associations and memories are created to retune the body and reset the brain.

Overarching learning goal

Cultivation of the gentle art of compassionate awareness: helping children to make kind choices for the self, others and the world.

Program intentions

- Introduce children to the marvellous, creative properties of their own bodies and minds
- Provide creative, play-based experiences to grow awareness of self and others
- Promote self-discovery and a growing sense of making good choices in life
- Help children apply the principles of Mindfulness to daily life

The brain loves novelty – a variety of resources, concepts and activities to fully engage children, light up neural pathways and build positive, connected networks are included in the program. Sessions include creative opportunities to explore ways of engaging the senses to embrace all learning styles and to connect to the heart and mind of each child.

Structure
of sessions

The format of each session is as follows:

Title of Inquiry: the learning focus of the session.

Teacher Preparation: this provides you with learning intentions, resources, focus words and tips for the session.

Resources: a selection of simple, accessible props and teaching aids bring the program to life and fully engages children. The saying 'a picture speaks a thousand words' is true!

There is no substitute for first-hand experience. Seeing, hearing, touching, smelling and feeling things encourages full engagement, creating tangible experiences for all children. Taste is a wonderful sense to connect to as well. However, given all the difficulties with food allergies, I have not included these experiences in this program. If your group does not have any food challenges, and you would like to share taste experiences, go ahead! You could use all kinds of contrasts with sour/sweet/salty/bitter flavours, as well as the smells, appearances and textures of food. Using novel, creative teaching aids can make your Mindfulness sessions more memorable and they also make sessions a lot more fun to share.

To make it easier for you to use this program, I have listed all the resources in a separate section and included informative notes. A list of required resources is also included in each session.

Focus Words: key words for discussion can help children to understand the purpose of each session, and to build a 'Mindful Vocabulary'.

Character Strengths: the program provides a perfect opportunity to introduce the concept of personal 'Strengths'. To find out more, visit the 'Values in Action Classification of Character Strengths' and discover your top strengths:
https://www.viacharacter.org/www/character-strengths

There are 24 VIA Character Strengths. Some of the terms used for these strengths are difficult for young children to understand. Consequently, I have made some alternative suggestions.

The overarching character strengths that lie at the heart of this program are curiosity and creativity.

There are many opportunities for character strengths to be highlighted and explored through characters in stories and discussions about choices, as well as incidental opportunities to remind children of universal qualities and strengths.

Delivery of Session: this provides a learning context and suggested 'scripts' for the session. Please do not feel that you need to 'rote learn' these, or read from them, but rather use them as a guide.

You will see that the structure of the lessons is inquiry-based. Learning comes alive when children fully engage and participate. The purpose of each session is for children to make their own Mindful discoveries.

Mindful Movement: the late, great neurologist, Oliver Sacks, identified the sense of proprioception (meaning holistic body awareness; involving spatial awareness, balance and co-ordination) as more important than all the other senses put together. All kinds of suggestions have been made to connect children with playful ideas and imagery and to spark their interest. Songs have been suggested to combine music with movement, enriching the experiences offered and enhancing the whole-body connection. Simple movement practices can literally rewire the brain, helping it to return to a state of harmony and balance.

Short, **Mindful 'movement rituals'**, for greetings, transitions and to highlight focus, are combined with longer practices that involve creative movement and dance. 'Mindful Movement' can be integrated into your day.

Sharing Circle: in this section there are suggested questions you can use to promote inquiry and participation, labelled as 'Q' (questions you ask) and 'A' (possible answers). Possible responses you may wish to add, or use as prompts to draw out more ideas, have been included. *Suggested responses have been provided to support children's answers and should only be used if necessary or desired. It is important to give children encouragement and time to reflect and contribute their own ideas.*

Quiet Inner Awareness/Mindful Meditation: *the most important prerequisite for teaching Meditation is investment in your own personal practice. There is no substitute for experience. Commitment to practice, with the support of a mentor or teacher, will fully prepare you to share Meditations with confidence and ease.*

In each session of the program, 'yin and yang' practices of movement and stillness exist side by side. Most children readily engage with and enjoy the movement practices. For some, it can take a bit longer to embrace stillness practices. For many young people, and older ones too, being quiet and still can seem strange at first. Often life can be so crammed full of non-stop stimulation, noise and activity that states of repose and non-doing can seem abnormal.

Consequently, it is important to have a playful approach to these practices. Creative images, metaphors and movements can draw children into Meditation with a sense of both fun and relevance. In time, these approaches help children to befriend inner awareness and stillness.

Neurologically, directing and sustaining attention 'turbo-charges' neurons in the frontal cortex. Intentional, purposeful Mindful Meditation practices effectively develop attention skills.

Before the 'Inner Awareness/Mindful Meditation' practices, remind children that this is a special opportunity to take very good care of their bodies and minds. Just as babies and young animals need a safe, quiet place to rest and grow, in cots, caves and nests, so do their bodies and minds! The difference between meditating and going to bed and dozing off to sleep, is that they are actively practising their noticing skills when they meditate.

When you lead these practices, take your time. It is helpful to speak slowly and clearly, creating space to allow children time to process and reflect on their experiences (*as indicated by '…'*).

It is very important not to impose these practices on children. Using coercion and punishment is entirely inappropriate and unhelpful. The best approach is to *offer an invitation* for children to join in and share the practices. If, for whatever reason, children are not ready, or do not wish to co-operate or participate, it is best to give them the choice of sitting out. They can choose another quiet activity, such as looking at books or drawing, remembering that they cannot disturb the group and understanding that when they do feel ready, they are very welcome to return to the group.

After the session, you may like to ask children what they noticed and to thank them for sharing. It is important not to judge responses and to reassure children that everyone has different and unique experiences in Meditation.

For audio files see page xxiii.

I have worked with children with special needs for many years. Importantly, I have also worked with children who have suffered trauma and abuse. Such experiences have informed my content and sequence of activities.

It is vital to offer safe focal points for children. A play-based approach with an attitude of curiosity provides a secure template. The sessions in this program take children through a range of experiences from external to internal focus. With children who have experienced trauma or abuse, it is very important to progress gently and slowly and initially, *help them discover neutral anchor points* (through the whole body, feet and hands and external senses of sight, sound and smell), before carefully venturing to explore visceral sensations of the breath, touch and inner sensations.

Being present, with a mind-set of compassionate curiosity, is the most important skill to practice in these sessions. Years ago, a young boy who had experienced abuse participated in a six-session course with me. For the first four sessions his safe place was under the table. Within the security of his own secure space, he remained completely engaged and attentive, even exploring his own version of practices in the confined space. My heart leapt in session five when he chose to 'come out' and join the group for the final two sessions.

Colleagues who work with traumatized children have encouraged them to find their own safe way to practice Meditation … inside cardboard boxes, under blankets and in the Yoga 'Child Pose', until they are ready to venture out to explore other options.

List of resources for sessions

I n every sense, *you* are the most important resource for this program. Being in a kind, calm, Mindful 'shape' and 'inner state' is the greatest gift you can bring to each session and each moment with children.

Throughout the program, suggestions have been made to enrich the learning experience, including the use of a variety of visual aids, props, books, stories and music.

A special note on music

Neuroscientific research has demonstrated the positive effects of music on both humans and animals.

Music connects to many parts of the brain: emotional (feelings and moods), cognitive (thinking) and motor (movement). Music builds memories, connecting to more areas of the brain than language – and this connection is effortless.

Music has a magical effect on young bodies and minds: calming, settling and soothing. Tempos and rhythms synchronize and harmonize bodies, hearts and minds and seamlessly unite everyone in a shared experience.

Suggestions for music and songs are included to support the Mindful Movements and activities. However, you can use whatever music you think will work best for the children in your care.

Speaking Stick: This option comes from Native American Indian traditions – only the person holding the stick has the right to speak. I have found that using the stick effortlessly enables alert, respectful active listening, while teaching children about being patient, sharing and taking turns. You could use any smooth, beautiful piece of wood. Ornaments, smooth rocks and large shells can also be used, but I find that the stick is very effective – it feels a bit like a toy microphone and encourages children to sit up and speak with authority!

Wooden Artists' Mannequin: Mannequins are a fantastic way to show children some of the countless shapes our bodies can make. It also helps children to understand that when the shape of the body changes, so do our feelings and moods. All kinds of different 'inner states' of feelings, moods and emotions can be suggested just by twisting the body into different angles, tilting the head or closing and opening the arms and legs.

Glitter Bottles: Over the years that I have worked with children, this has been one of the most effective, simple and popular visual aids. When the bottle is vigorously shaken, the glitter whirls around like a storm! Then, when the bottle is placed on a still, flat surface, all the glitter slowly, gracefully sinks to the bottom and the water returns to its former clarity. This creates a wonderful metaphor for our states of mind: busy and chaotic, or calm and clear.

You can make your own bottles using either a clean, clear glass jar or a plastic water bottle. Add a spoonful of multi-coloured glitter, one drop of dishwashing detergent, a generous tablespoon of rice malt syrup or glycerine and then add water. Screw the lid on tightly, shake vigorously and your glitter bottle is ready to use.

Pictures/puppets/soft toys: Lizard, Monkey and Giraffe.

Diagram/image of cross-section of brain and an **image of a human cell**

Charts/pictures of muscular/skeletal systems

Large square of stretch material (like lycra) to create a mini-trampoline

Three Bowls: one big, one average, one small.

Singing bowl/chimes/triangle

Selection of natural objects: a range of different feathers, leaves, wood, grasses, seed pods, flowers, spices, shells, rocks etc.

Mystery objects: A variety of soft or hard little 'mystery' objects to place inside socks or small pieces of material. For example: sponges, cotton balls, rubber bands, cotton reels, little plastic toys, tiny bottles/jars, spoons, buttons, seed pods, etc.

Pictures: nature scenes, families, pets.

Paper, coloured pencils, crayons

The Mindful Gift Box: any colourful gift box, along with assorted coloured lengths of ribbon or small pieces of different coloured fabric.

Glass 'jewels': small, coloured glass beads.

Drawings/pictures/blocks of basic shapes and shapes found in nature: squares, rectangles, circles, triangles.

Hula hoops/circles of soft, cool-coloured material/yoga mats

List of music

- 'The Sanctuary', Peter Roberts
- 'Wiyathul', Geoffrey Gurrumul Yunupingu
- 'Clarinet Concerto in A Major, Adagio', Mozart
- 'Flight of the Bumblebee', Rimsky-Korsakov
- 'Shepherd Moons', Enya
- 'Somewhere Over the Rainbow', Israel Kamakawiwo'ole
- 'Air Concerto: Orchestral Suite No. 3', Bach
- 'Canon in D', Pachelbel
- 'Happy', Pharrell Williams
- 'The Moonlight Sonata', Piano Sonata #14 in C Sharp, Beethoven
- 'Carnival of the Animals', Saint-Saëns
- 'Gymnopédies No. 1. Lent et Douloureux', Erik Satie
- 'Daintree Rainforest', Ken Davis
- 'Kodama Tree Spirit', Jane Rutter
- 'This Little Light of Mine', Bible Songs for Children
- 'What a Wonderful World', Louis Armstrong
- 'La Petite Fille De La Mer', Vangelis

- 'Oh, The Places You'll Go!' by Dr. Seuss
- 'My Many Colored Days' by Dr. Seuss
- 'Slowly, Slowly, Slowly, said the Sloth' by Eric Carle
- 'Goldilocks and the Three Bears' by Robert Southey
- 'Where's Wally?' by Martin Handford
- 'Wild About Shapes' by Jeremie Fischer
- Escher artwork books
- 'Belonging' and other books by Jeannie Baker
- 'Spot the Difference' cartoons

MP3 audio files of Quiet Inner Awareness/Mindful Meditation practices recordings by Janet Etty-Leal can be purchased on the Meditation Capsules website:

https://www.meditationcapsules.shop

PART ONE

Noticing the body

"Enjoy your body, use it every way you can. Don't be afraid of it, or what other people think of it, it's the greatest instrument you'll ever own." — KURT VONNEGUT JR.

Character Strengths
- Love of Learning
- Curiosity
- Creativity
- Open-Mindedness
- Kindness

The ability to pay attention underpins everything we do in life. It is a prerequisite for learning, achievement and relationships.

Mindfulness is about waking up and remembering what matters. Noticing how the mind wanders and ways to return it to where it needs to be in this moment. Noticing what the body is feeling and what it needs and connecting to other people and understanding their needs. Waking up to kind, wise choices, moment by moment.

The most important place to start noticing and paying attention is the body. Helping children establish a caring sense of responsibility and appreciation for the amazing instrument of their body and mind gives them a gift for a lifetime.

The program is designed to take children on a sequential path of personal discovery. Sessions progress from simple focus points to more complex and intriguing concepts, extending skills of awareness.

Session 1 supports the character strengths of curiosity and love of learning. Suggestions for teaching aids and props to promote engagement and concentration are introduced. Children can discover how paying attention literally 'lights up' our mind, as we learn, connect and enjoy life more. Experiences include noticing the body as it moves and enjoying feelings and sensations in the body when we give it the special treat of returning to a state of rest and stillness.

Session 2 supports the character strengths of curiosity and creativity. Focus is placed on shapes, engaging children in noticing basic geometric examples and recognizing all kinds of shapes in the world around them. Awareness is then focused on all the different shapes that our bodies can make. Wooden artists' mannequins provide an excellent visual aid for this purpose. Mindful movements and meditation practice engage children in first-hand experiences of the changing shapes their bodies can create.

Session 3 supports the character strengths of open-mindedness, curiosity and kindness. The beam of focus shifts from outer awareness to inner awareness – from outer shapes to inner states. Experiences are designed to highlight how quickly the body can change, both within and without. Simple practices create personal experiences for children to discover their ability to pause, notice, and calm and soothe their bodies and minds internally and externally.

Ways of noticing

TEACHER PREPARATION

RESOURCES

- Speaking Stick
- A small torch/flashlight
- Drawing or picture of a pause symbol
- **Props:** Pictures, flowers and other specimens from nature to support the lesson
- **Book:** 'Oh, The Places You'll Go!' by Dr. Seuss
- **Music:** 'The Sanctuary' by Peter Roberts for the Mindful Movement Ritual

FOCUS WORDS

notice
attention
senses
pause
now
space
base

CHARACTER STRENGTHS

Love of learning, curiosity

LEARNING GOAL

Noticing how and why we pay attention

TIPS

Before the session, try out the 'Mindful Movement', experiencing the benefits of taking some time to notice feeling aligned and relaxed.

The program is inquiry-based, encouraging children to interact, engage and find answers themselves by actively participating. During the sharing circle, you are guiding this inquiry process.

Have a look at 'Oh, The Places You'll Go!' by Dr. Seuss and decide which pages you would like to share with the children (it is a long book).

Remember to be mindful yourself by smiling, establishing eye contact with each child and speaking slowly and clearly.

The aim of this session is to bring Mindfulness to life through 'first-hand' experiences that help children to befriend, respect and value their bodies and minds.

Mindfulness skills nurture ways for children to be curious, attentive and fully connected to the richness of each moment.

DELIVERY OF SESSION

Introduction for students

Share the following in your own words:

"Mindfulness is a way to take good care of our body and mind: to notice what it is doing and feeling and to develop wise ways to use it."

"Noticing is a skill that we can practice so our mind works even better! We can notice what we need to be happy and make good choices every day."

"The skill of noticing helps us to grow an important strength, which is the love of learning. Every day there is always something new that we can learn."

"Some of the first lines of 'Oh, The Places You'll Go!' by Dr. Seuss are: "You have brains in your head. You have feet in your shoes. You can steer yourself any direction you choose.""

"When we practise being Mindful we make the most of our body and mind. We practise paying careful attention, moment by moment, so we can grow a strong mind. We need strong minds for all the places we will go … and all the things we will do!"

"Let's start noticing right now with our bodies."

Invite children to take off their shoes.

SHARING CIRCLE

Pass the Speaking Stick to a volunteer for each answer.

Q. What does the word 'notice' mean?

A. When we notice, we are focusing and paying attention.

Q. Why do we need to pause to notice well?

A. When we pause, we stop what we are doing and become still, so we can notice ... and I notice now, that everyone is noticing me and what I am saying.

Torch or Flashlight: use this as a visual example. Turn it on to demonstrate how it brings our attention to wherever it goes.

"This torch helps us to really notice: it 'lights up' whatever it lands on, so we can see clearly, focus and pay attention."

During the questioning sequence, invite children to share their favourite things.

Q. Which parts of our body do we notice with? (Use your hands to gesture to different parts of the body that connect with senses).

A. We use parts of the body that are connected to our 'senses': eyes, ears, mouth, nose, skin on our hands/feet/all over our bodies.

Q. What do we notice with our eyes?

A. We see things like colours, shapes, people, toys, trees and animals.

Q. What do we notice with our ears?

A. We hear things like voices, music, footsteps, machines, cars, birds, wind and rain.

Q. What do we notice with our mouth?

A. We taste and feel things. Feelings such as: happiness and sadness. Tasting things such as: cheese, bread, vegetables, fruit, ice cream and chocolate.

Q. What do we notice with our nose?

A. We smell things such as: flowers, chocolate, pizza, grass, fruit and perfume.

Q. What do we notice with our skin – hands, feet, body?

A. We feel things such as: water, sun, clothes, play dough, sand, soft toys and hugging others.

"Noticing **is very important**. Practising the skill of noticing helps us grow the wonderful character strength of curiosity. Being curious keeps our mind sharp and alert. When we pause and notice, important messages travel to our brain. Every time we carefully notice, we are learning and becoming wiser."

"When we pause to notice our body, we can help it feel stronger, calmer and happier."

*Use the wooden artists' mannequin to illustrate how different angles through the back, shoulders and head, and different spaces and shapes with arms and legs completely change the feeling of the body.

"Now, which means in this very moment, we can enjoy being quiet so that we can practise noticing how our body is feeling … and ways we can be kind to it."

MINDFUL MOVEMENT

Making Shapes

Music: 'The Sanctuary' by Peter Roberts.

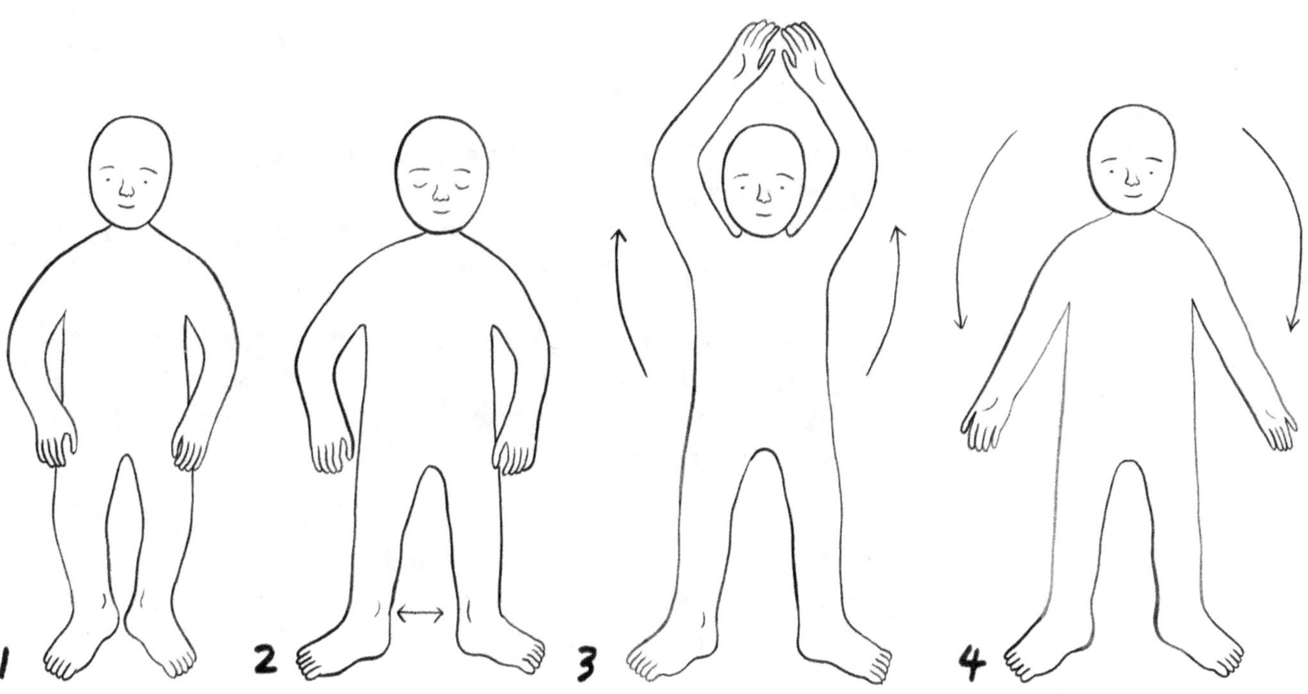

"We can do some simple practices to notice our body changing shape now.

1 **"Let's begin by bringing our feet so close together that your legs feel like a 'sandwich'.** Perhaps your body feels like a stiff, hard pole! … Notice how tricky it is to move your back and arms with your legs stuck together."

2 **"Now, let's notice what it feels like when your feet step open** … just wide enough to make a space for a strong base underneath your body … just enough space to help you feel strong and balanced."

3 **"Now, notice your breathing** and taking a big, deep breath … let your arms lift up as you breathe in … all the way up above your head … stretching up above you and notice as you breathe out … they can just float down again … all the way down to rest beside your body."

4 **"You can let them do that again** … just letting your arms lift up as you breathe in … all the way up above your head … stretching up above you … and notice as you breathe out … your arms just float down again, to rest beside your body."

"Now, notice your body change shape, as you let it sit down quietly on the floor."

QUIET INNER AWARENESS/MINDFUL MEDITATION

Lying down practice

"Find a space, and a place, for your body to rest and be quiet … and lie down on your back. You might even like to let your eyes have a rest … just letting them close gently down when they are ready."

"Every day we practise noticing. We notice how we get dressed (so our clothes are not inside out and upside down!). We notice what we are eating and how we wash ourselves. We notice when we are doing things and making things."

"Our body needs us to notice it as well, so that it can calm down. So now, notice your body becoming still … letting your feet rest and be still … and then letting your legs rest and become still too … Letting your hands be still … so that your arms can become still … Letting your body be still and quiet … feeling the softness flowing all the way along your back and up into your shoulders. Notice your neck resting with your head …"

"Now you can **notice sounds** around you … Perhaps you can notice sounds like birds outside … or the wind … or rain and perhaps you can hear people in the building as they talk and walk around …"

"Now **notice the touch** of the floor right underneath you … feeling how quiet, hard and strong the floor is … as it holds all of your body … and just letting your body be … There is nothing that your body has to do right now … Letting it be soft and calm … Noticing your body as it soaks up all the quiet and stillness … Just letting your body deeply, deeply rest …"

Children spend a few moments in stillness and silence to fully experience what they are feeling now.

"Taking your time … slowly, gently begin to move the body again with a slow, big stretch through your arms … and legs … and then you might like to roll over and lie on your side for a while … until you are ready to slowly return to sitting up."

MINDFUL MOVEMENT / RITUAL

A 'Mindful Farewell' for the session

Invite everyone to return to a cross-legged sitting position.

"Bring your hands to press together (with palms facing in a 'prayer position') in a tight shape in front of your heart. Breathe in … and as you slowly breathe out … let your hands change into a soft shape, with all your fingers softening to create a soft space inside, just like the shape of a cocoon. Inside a cocoon, a butterfly is forming … just like the beautiful changes inside us when we pause and make kind choices."

"**Hold your kind 'cocoon' hands in front of your heart.**
Breathe in ... and as you breathe out, **bow in respect and
kindness for yourself** ... Then, breathe in ... and breathe out
... and **bow with respect and kindness for others** ... Lastly,
breathe in ... and breathe out, and **bow with respect and
kindness for nature and the world**."

"Now, let your 'butterfly' hands open ... and smile ... sharing
your beautiful smile with everyone ... and wave or twinkle
all your fingers to spread your kindness to every person in
the group."

SESSION 2
What is your outer shape?

TEACHER PREPARATION

RESOURCES

- Speaking Stick
- Wooden Artists' Mannequin
- **Drawings/pictures/blocks of basic shapes and shapes found in nature:** squares, rectangles, circles, triangles
- Charts/pictures of muscular/skeletal systems
- **Music:** 'Wiyathul' by Geoffrey Gurrumul Yunupingu for the Mindful Movement Ritual

FOCUS WORDS

muscles
bones
squares
rectangles
circles
triangles

CHARACTER STRENGTHS

Curiosity, creativity

LEARNING GOAL

To notice what 'shape' you are in

TIPS

Take a few moments to tune in to your own body, to notice what shape you are in before the lesson (or whenever you can). Notice feelings of tightness and stiffness and realise the benefits of stretching with the breath to let go of tension.

Practise making a variety of shapes for the Mindful Movement Activity before commencing the session.

S hapes provide a 'vocabulary of form' for children. This session helps children transfer awareness and knowledge of shapes to their own body.

A sense of different shapes is developed through discussion and Mindful Movements with the 'Simon Says' game.

DELIVERY OF SESSION

MINDFUL MOVEMENT / RITUAL

Music: 'Wiyathul' by Geoffrey Gurrumul Yunupingu.

Introduce a 'Mindful Pause', beginning the session with this practice.

"Stand in your space. Create a strong base with your feet and legs to hold your body. Let your back make a strong, straight shape ... and let your head feel light ... like it is a balloon floating on a string ... Take a big, deep breath and let your hands float up to come together in a point above your head. As you breathe out, let your hands slide down, and let one rest on your heart and the other on your tummy. Softly, quietly, say to yourself: 'Thank you body ... I will practise noticing what is kind for you now.' Then, let your hands give you a big hug."

Share the following in your own words:

"Everything in life is made up of shapes. Some of them are big and some are small. Some of them are hard shapes and some are soft shapes. Some of the shapes we see are human-made and others we can notice in nature."

SHARING CIRCLE

Pass the Speaking Stick to a volunteer for each answer.

Q. What shapes can you see now in this room?

A. Straight, thin, thick, square, round, triangular.

(Show some examples of shapes using pictures or objects).

Q. Which parts of the body make it change shape?

A. Bones and muscles.

"Let's notice the shapes our faces can make with our mouth, eyes and eyebrows." (Point to these). "Show me the mean, scary shapes your face can make! What do these shapes *feel like*? Would you want to be stuck with these shapes?"

"Let's notice the happy, kind shapes our faces can make. What do these feel like?"

"We can notice that some shapes feel stiff, tight and hard, and other shapes feel soft, loose and light."

ACTIVITY

"Creativity is a wonderful character strength. Let's remember that we all have creative bodies that can make all kinds of shapes."

"Let's notice what shapes our whole body can make now! Standing up and finding your space, we will notice how the body changes shape: it's just like playing 'Simon Says' … but no one will 'go out'!"

Be Very, Very Tall	*Be Very, Very Small*
Be a Pointy Pencil	*Be a Floppy Doll*
Be Square	*Be Round*
Be a Rock	*Be a Feather*
Be a Brick	*Be a Cloud*
Be a Door	*Be a Bouncy Ball*

Q. Who noticed that when you change shape, your feelings changed as well?

A. (Invite responses from children).

QUIET INNER AWARENESS/MINDFUL MEDITATION

Sitting practice

"Choose your own quiet space in which to sit down. Feel your body change shape from being tall and straight, to becoming smaller as you sit ... **Notice your body settling into your 'sitting shape'** – with your legs crossed and your back straight ..."

"Pretend that there is a beautiful, strong silver ribbon attached to our spine and back that goes all the way up to the clouds ... holding your back still and straight so that your head feels as if it is floating over your calm, strong body ..."

"**Now notice your hands** ... stretching your hands out in front so you can see them ... and feel them change shape: make them tight and wide open, like starfish ... and then just let them feel like jellyfish ... soft and floppy ... let's do that again ... tight starfish hands ... and then loose, jellyfish hands ... They might like to float down to find a resting place on your legs now ..." (Pause to allow time for students to fully experience this awareness).

"**Let's notice your eyes now** ... open them wide ... and then just let your eyelids change shape ... slowly and gently ... becoming softer and softer ... so they feel like they just want to close down ... Just letting them rest ... softly closing your eyelids for a while ... so your eyes can rest."

"**Let's notice your shoulders now** ... feel them changing shape: holding them tight and stiff under your ears ... and as you breathe out ... just let them drop into a soft, easy, round shape ... with your arms resting beside you ..."

"**Now just sit quietly and still, with your body in a comfortable, peaceful shape** ... Let it rest for a while ... enjoying being in a gentle, soft shape."

Children spend a few moments in stillness and silence to fully experience what they are feeling now.

"When your body is ready, let it slowly, gently move again … with a slow, big stretch through your arms and legs … and allow your eyes to open."

MINDFUL MOVEMENT / RITUAL

A 'Mindful Farewell' for the session

Invite everyone to return to a cross-legged sitting position.

"Bring your hands to press together (with palms facing in a 'prayer position') in a tight shape in front of your heart. Breathe in … and as you slowly breathe out … let your hands change into a soft shape, with all your fingers softening to create a soft space inside, just like the shape of a cocoon. Inside a cocoon, a butterfly is forming … just like the beautiful changes inside us when we pause and make kind choices."

"**Hold your kind 'cocoon' hands in front of your heart.** Breathe in … and as you breathe out, **bow in respect and kindness for yourself** … Then, breathe in … and breathe out … and **bow with respect and kindness for others** … Lastly, breathe in … and breathe out, and **bow with respect and kindness for nature and the world**."

"Now, let your 'butterfly' hands open … and smile … sharing your beautiful smile with everyone … and wave or twinkle all your fingers to spread your kindness to every person in the group."

SESSION 3
What is your inner state?

TEACHER PREPARATION

RESOURCES

- Speaking Stick
- Glitter Bottle
- **Book:** 'My Many Colored Days' by Dr. Seuss
- **Music:** 'Clarinet Concerto in A Major, Adagio' by Mozart for the Mindful Movement Rituals and Activity, 'Flight of the Bumblebee' by Rimsky-Korsakov for Activity

FOCUS WORDS

kindness
curiosity
states
feelings
emotions

CHARACTER STRENGTHS

Curiosity, open-mindedness, kindness

LEARNING GOAL

To notice what 'state' we are in

TIPS

Begin to practise pausing to notice, with kindness and curiosity, the ever-changing 'inner weather map' of your own inner experience. Remember that Mindfulness is not about judging. It is about noticing and connecting to kind choices, and ways to return to balance and harmony.

Practise the Mindful Rituals yourself, so that you can demonstrate them to the children in your care.

Spend some time reading the Dr. Seuss book and listening to the contrasting music and note how your body responds.

This program leads children on a sequential journey of discovery: to notice, know and befriend themselves and others. Children are guided on a journey of becoming 'their own best friend', noticing with kindness and curiosity (not judgement) the ever-changing shapes, states, and feelings inside their bodies and minds. In time, this knowledge will help them notice and understand what state other people are experiencing.

In this stage of the journey, children may start to notice subtle states of feeling and sensation.

DELIVERY OF SESSION

MINDFUL MOVEMENT / RITUAL 1

Music: 'Clarinet Concerto in A Major, Adagio' by Mozart.

Introduce a 'Mindful Pause', beginning the session with this practise.

"Stand in your space. Create a strong base with your feet and legs to hold your body … Let your back make a strong, straight shape … and let your head feel light … like it is a balloon floating on a string … Take a big, deep breath and let your hands float up to come together in a point above

your head. As you breathe out, let your hands slide down, and let one rest on your heart and the other on your tummy. Softly, quietly, say to yourself: 'Thank you body … I will practise noticing what is kind for you now.' Then, let your hands give you a big hug."

Now flow to the practice below.

MINDFUL MOVEMENT / RITUAL 2

Mindful greeting

"Now, take another big, deep breath and let your hands float up to come together in a point above your head.

1 "As you breathe out, let your hands slide down, and pause in front of **your forehead**: breathe gently and notice **kind thoughts**."

2 "Take another big, deep breath … and as you breathe out, let your hands slide down to pause in front of **your mouth**: breathe gently and notice **kind words**."

3 "Take another big, deep breath … and as you breathe out, let your hands slide down to pause in front of **your heart**: breathe gently and notice **kind feelings** … for yourself, others and the world."

*Practice courtesy of Catherine Shepard, Still Point Yoga

Share the following in your own words:

"When we pause, and notice carefully, we can realise that our bodies are always changing shape. We can see this with our eyes. And inside our bodies feelings are always changing too. We can notice the different 'states' that can be inside our body."

(Use the glitter bottle as a visual example of how quickly the body can change from a clear, calm and still inner state, to a busy, chaotic state … and then gently return to its original clear, calm state).

Read 'My Many Colored Days' by Dr. Seuss.

SHARING CIRCLE

Pass the Speaking Stick to a volunteer for each answer.

Q. Invite children to share what different colours might 'feel like' for them?

A. Happy, sad, cheerful, cross, angry, shy, quiet, loud, little, big (connect colours to the 'moods or states' we can feel).

Help children to understand that these 'states' change often – they come and go, just like the weather. Explain to the children that our bodies are like big 'containers' of lots of feelings that come and go all day, every day. Emphasise the need to notice to take care of these feelings, and to help our bodies return to feeling calm and happy.

ACTIVITY

Music: 'Flight of the Bumblebee' by Rimsky-Korsakov; and 'Clarinet Concerto in A Major, Adagio' by Mozart.

Invite children to have fun and discover what shapes and states they notice when their bodies move with the different music. Alternate back and forth between the two pieces of music.

Pause between each change and ask children to notice how they are feeling.

Invite children to share any feelings they noticed with the different music and movements.

Finish the activity by listening to Mozart. Invite children to feel their bodies turning into soft, round shapes, finding a space and place to be quiet and still on the floor.

QUIET INNER AWARENESS/MINDFUL MEDITATION

Standing to lying down

"Choose your own quiet space for your body and stand still in this space. Feel your feet create a strong base to hold your body ... Let your back make a strong, straight shape ... just letting your head feel light ... like it is a balloon ... floating lightly over your body. Let your shoulders be soft ... and let your arms feel floppy and loose, as they rest beside you ... Take some time to notice what this shape feels like ..."

"Slowly, quietly changing shape now – shifting from standing **tall and still** ... to sinking down ... and down ... bending your knees until you are in a **squatting** shape, with your strong legs bent over your strong feet ... and your hands resting on the floor ... Notice what this shape feels like for you ..."

"Then tip forward until you are **kneeling** ... with your feet folded flat underneath you ... your back straight and strong ... and your hands resting gently and quietly on your lap ... Take time to notice what this shape feels like ..."

"Now, slowly and quietly, changing shape again to a **forward stretch** ... Letting your hands stretch out along the floor ... and letting your body follow ... until your body rests against your legs ... and your head rests down against the floor ... Notice what this shape feels like ..."

"Then, when you are ready, **roll over to quietly lie flat on the floor on your back** ... Feel your body resting softly against the floor ... Noticing what this shape feels like ... and how your body feels now ..."

Children spend a few moments in stillness and silence to fully experience what they are feeling now.

"When your body is ready, let it slowly, gently move again ... with a slow, big stretch through your arms and legs ... and then you might like to roll over and lie on your side for a while ... until you are ready to slowly return to sitting up."

A 'Mindful Farewell' for the session

Invite everyone to return to a cross-legged sitting position.

"Bring your hands to press together (with palms facing in a 'prayer position') in a tight shape in front of your heart. Breathe in … and as you slowly breathe out … let your hands change into a soft shape, with all your fingers softening to create a soft space inside, just like the shape of a cocoon. Inside a cocoon, a butterfly is forming … just like the beautiful changes inside us when we pause and make kind choices."

"**Hold your kind 'cocoon' hands in front of your heart**. Breathe in … and as you breathe out, **bow in respect and kindness for yourself** … Then, breathe in … and breathe out … and **bow with respect and kindness for others** … Lastly, breathe in … and breathe out, and **bow with respect and kindness for nature and the world**."

"Now, let your 'butterfly' hands open … and smile … sharing your beautiful smile with everyone … and wave or twinkle all your fingers to spread your kindness to every person in the group."

Noticing your choices

"To live is to choose. But to choose well, you must know who you are and what you stand for, where you want to go and why you want to get there." — KOFI ANNAN

Character Strengths

- Curiosity
- Perspective
- Prudence
- Fairness
- Self-control

If we trace the origins of Mindfulness, the original meaning of the word, sourced from the Pali scripts more than 2,000 years old, is translated as 'to remember'.

In the busyness of life, it is easy to forget all kinds of things. We forget where our attention is, where we have put things, what we are doing, thinking and feeling. We forget what really matters. It is easy to live in an 'automatic pilot' state of mind, fuelled by old habits and mind-sets.

As we practise creating some space, with a sense of 'Mindful Punctuation', we can remember kind anchor points for awareness, such as space for curiosity and reflection and time to remember that we always have choices.

The sessions in Part 4 amplify the choices we can make.

Session 4 supports the character strengths of curiosity, prudence, perspective and self-control (feel free to use the words you feel are appropriate for your students). The concept of pausing is introduced, to help children realise the importance of a quiet space to notice more carefully and effectively and

to create spaces for wise choices. The book '"Slowly, Slowly, Slowly," said the Sloth' brings awareness to the importance of being quiet and doing things slowly, aligning with the character strength of prudence – being careful, sensible and wise.

Session 5 supports the character strengths of perspective (understanding) and self-control (self-care, awareness). Puppets could be used to link to the Eric Carle story from the previous session. You will find this session includes a very lively activity! Children can discover the links between animals, the human body and the brain. Awareness of the breath is introduced, with movements, leading to quiet and still meditation practice.

Session 6 supports the same character strengths as Session 5, as well as the strength of fairness, when they reflect on Goldilocks choices! The story 'Goldilocks and the Three Bears' provides insight for choices. Children can then enjoy experiencing 'Just Right' choices as they move and notice feet, legs, hands, arms, spine, shoulders and heads with the song 'Happy' by Pharrell Williams. Quiet, still 'Just Right' choices are then explored in the meditation practice.

Space to pause

TEACHER PREPARATION

RESOURCES

Refer to 'Resources' list

- Speaking Stick
- Drawing/picture of a pause symbol
- Hula hoops/circles of soft, cool-coloured material/yoga mats
- **Book:** '"Slowly, Slowly, Slowly," said the Sloth' by Eric Carle
- **Music:** 'Shepherd Moons' by Enya for the Mindful Movement Ritual and 'Somewhere Over the Rainbow' by Israel Kamakawiwo'ole, for the Mindful Movement Activity with hula hoops

FOCUS WORDS

pause
present
space
choice

CHARACTER STRENGTHS

Curiosity, prudence (careful, sensible, wisdom), perspective (understanding), self-control (self-care, awareness)

LEARNING GOAL

To create space to notice

TIPS

It is important to become familiar with the music and to experience the movements before you introduce them to the children. Spend some time absorbing the text and pictures of the book, so you can guide inquiry with the children.

Begin to practise just slowing down a little in life (walking, moving, speaking) to experience for yourself what this feels like.

Part 2 of the program builds on the foundation of body awareness in Part 1, guiding children to 'join awareness dots' in life. Progression is moving from gross motor skill awareness, to finer, more subtle levels of noticing and experiencing feelings and changes in daily life.

For many people, life is lived at high speed: rushing from one place and one activity to another. This session brings attention to the vital skill of pausing: slowing down and being quiet and still, so that we can notice what really matters inside and outside. Creating space, every day, to develop a sharper, clearer mind.

DELIVERY OF SESSION

MINDFUL MOVEMENT / RITUAL 1

Music: 'Shepherd Moons' by Enya.

Introduce a 'Mindful Pause', beginning the session with this practice.

"Stand in your space. Create a strong base with your feet and legs to hold your body. Let your back make a strong, straight shape … and let your head feel light … like it is a balloon floating on a string … Take a big, deep breath and let your hands float up to come together in a point above your head. As you breathe out, let your hands slide down,

and let one rest on your heart and the other on your tummy. Softly, quietly, say to yourself: 'Thank you body … I will practise noticing what is kind for you now.' Then, let your hands give you a big hug."

Now flow to the practice below.

MINDFUL MOVEMENT / RITUAL 2

Mindful greeting

Music: 'The Sanctuary' by Peter Roberts.

"Now, take another big, deep breath and let your hands float up to come together in a point above your head."

1 "As you breathe out, let your hands slide down, and pause in front of **your forehead**: breathe gently and notice **kind thoughts**."

2 "Take another big, deep breath … and as you breathe out, let your hands slide down to pause in front of **your mouth**: breathe gently and notice **kind words**."

3 "Take another big, deep breath … and as you breathe out, let your hands slide down to pause in front of **your heart**: breathe gently and notice **kind feelings** … for yourself, others and the world."

Share the following in your own words:

"Mindfulness is a practice that 'shines a light on life' … just like a torch or flashlight shining on something. It helps us notice clearly and remember the kind choices we can make."

"Today we will notice why it is important to pause and slow down so that we can notice carefully." (Introduce the image of the pause symbol)."

Share the book with the children, pointing out any features you wish to highlight.

SHARING CIRCLE

Pass the Speaking Stick to a volunteer for each answer.

Q. What did you notice in this story?

A. (Prompt responses from children).

Q. Why is it important in your life to do some things slowly?

A. When we do things slowly and carefully, we can enjoy them more and take better care with what we are doing.

Q. Which things do you carry out in a better way when you do them slowly?

A. Getting dressed, eating, making things, climbing, doing puzzles, drawing, painting, cooking and listening.

Q. What does the word 'pause' mean?

A. A temporary stop.

Q. When do we use a pause?

A. When watching movies/DVDs, YouTube clips, between activities, to look and listen carefully … and when making choices in life: at home, in the Centre and the playground.

Explain that when we slow down … and stop, we make space for a pause, so that we can be present. Then, there is time and space to notice carefully and make good choices for ourselves, others and the world.

ACTIVITY

Music: 'Somewhere Over the Rainbow' by Israel Kamakawiwoʻole.

Place hula hoops/circles of material/yoga mats in spaces around the room.

Introduce this activity as a game, like 'Musical Chairs', or 'Musical Statues', but these are 'Quiet Spaces' and no one misses out!

Share the following in your own words:

"When the music plays, let your body enjoy moving in all kinds of happy ways. Let your hands and arms, feet and legs, and your whole body enjoy making different movements and shapes."

"The hula hoops/circles of material/yoga mats create special spaces to become quiet and still. When we pause, and stop in this space, we can choose a shape that our body would like to be in, to catch our breath and calm down. Your body might like to be in a standing shape, a squatting shape, a kneeling shape, a sitting shape or a lying down shape. You can try different shapes each time the music stops."

"At the end, when the music becomes softer and softer, choose a space in which you'd like to spend more quiet time."

Flow gently to stillness …

QUIET INNER AWARENESS/MINDFUL MEDITATION

Standing to sitting practice

"Find your space, and place, and let your body make a 'standing tall' shape. Then, notice your hands – let's make a 'Mindful Parachute' with our hands … Slowly breathe in and let your hands float up … and up … into the air beside you … until they have made a beautiful parachute shape above your head."

"Letting your shoulders be soft and loose … let your parachute lift you gently upwards … As you breathe out … feel yourself sinking down just a little bit, keeping your parachute hands and arms floating high above, feeling your knees softly bending …" (Repeat four times).

"Now, every time you breathe out, let your beautiful parachute bring you slowly, gently down to a safe, soft landing ... so your body can find its resting space ... When you are sitting quiet and still, let your soft, gentle 'parachute hands' come to land on you ... spreading softness and calm **through your head (pause) ... ears (pause) ... eyes (pause) ... just letting your eyes close down to feel your warm, soft hands ... nose (pause) ... mouth (pause) ... jaw (pause) ... neck (pause)** ... Your kind, caring, gentle hands sliding softly and gently down further ... until they slide down to **your chest (pause)** ... spreading more and more calmness and softness ... Let them **rest on your heart (pause) ... tummy (pause)** ... and finally ... your hands might like to come to **completely rest in your lap.**"

"Notice what's happening inside now ... feeling your whole body becoming soft like a sponge ... just enjoying being quiet and still ..."

Children spend a few moments in stillness and silence to fully experience what they are feeling now.

"Feel the breath slowly deepening ... and slowly 'wake up' your body with some stretching through your hands and arms ..."

MINDFUL MOVEMENT / RITUAL 3

A 'Mindful Farewell' for the session

Invite everyone to return to a cross-legged sitting position.

"Bring your hands to press together (with palms facing in a 'prayer position') in a tight shape in front of your heart. Breathe in ... and as you slowly breathe out ... let your hands change into a soft shape, with all your fingers softening to create a soft space inside, just like the shape of a cocoon. Inside a cocoon, a butterfly is forming ... just like the beautiful changes inside us when we pause and make kind choices."

"**Hold your kind 'cocoon' hands in front of your heart**.
Breathe in … and as you breathe out, **bow in respect and
kindness for yourself** … Then, breathe in … and breathe out
… and **bow with respect and kindness for others** … Lastly,
breathe in … and breathe out, and **bow with respect and
kindness for nature and the world**."

"Now, let your 'butterfly' hands open … and smile … sharing
your beautiful smile with everyone … and wave or twinkle
all your fingers to spread your kindness to every person in
the group."

SESSION 5
Breathing and the brain

TEACHER PREPARATION

RESOURCES

- Speaking Stick
- **Pictures/puppets/soft toys:** Lizard, Monkey and Giraffe
- **Stretch fabric:** for 'monkey mind' activities
- Balloon
- Diagram/image of cross-section of brain
- Image of a human cell
- **Music:** 'Air Concerto: Orchestral Suite No. 3' by Bach for the Mindful Movement Ritual and Activity

FOCUS WORDS

breath
cell
brain
choice

CHARACTER STRENGTHS

Perspective (understanding), self-control (self-care, awareness)

LEARNING GOAL

To notice the breath and how it connects to how our brain works and how we feel

TIPS

Become familiar with the locations of the key areas of the brain.

Occasionally pause to notice the patterns or states of your own breathing. Practise taking some time to straighten the spine and create space in the chest and body to allow for deep, connected breaths, experiencing the benefits for yourself.

Practise doing the Mindful Movement: 'Balloon Man'.

Breath is our connection with life and energy. In the past sessions, we have been building a 'body vocabulary' with the children – noticing different shapes and states the body can be in.

This session uses playful awareness to bring attention to the breath. It also connects to what state and shape the brain is in. The three parts of the brain are introduced:

- **'reptilian' brain** ('downstairs brain': cerebellum/brain stem – the oldest part of the brain) that keeps us alive and does lots of things, like moving muscles, managing breathing, swallowing, blinking and body functioning
- **limbic brain** which deals with emotions like happiness, fear, excitement and anger
- **frontal cortex** (the 'upstairs brain') located inside the forehead, which deals with our choices, decision making and planning, managing our emotions, self-understanding and social connection, as well as empathy and morality.

Animals are often used to represent these three functions of the brain. Often an owl is used to represent the frontal cortex. However, as this is a nocturnal creature and a predator (which may have scary associations for some children!) I prefer to use a giraffe, a gentle, passive omnivore that can see everything. It is important for children to realise that there are not 'good' and 'bad' areas of the brain. We need all parts of the brain to work well to keep us alive. When our brain gets out of balance, we need to remember that we can make wise, calm choices to care for it. The ability to be aware, pause and make Mindful choices helps us return the brain and the body to a state of harmony.

Getting into shape and connecting to the breath, so that it can deepen and gently slow down, is one of these important choices. It is certainly worth practising.

The suggested activity is a rowdy one – which children in my classes have adored (and begged to do it again years later). It involves the children sitting around the edge of a piece of stretch fabric (I use two: green for the first part, when rapid movements make the monkey 'lose his mind' and then a blue piece of fabric to calm monkey down with our slow breaths and hand movements).

The monkey is placed in the middle, with everyone holding the edges of the fabric. We let our hands move quickly up and down as we breathe quickly and watch the poor monkey 'losing his mind' … as he gets tossed all over the place (and usually is ejected from the fabric). To restore order, it is helpful to ask everyone to stand and do the Mindful Movement 'Balloon Man Practice'.

Then everyone can take their seat, and with deep, slow breaths and creating gentle 'waves' with their hands: breathing in as hands float up … and slowly sighing out the out-breath, as the hands float down again.

You can use the toy monkey to take turns on children's tummies as they calm down with the Meditation practice afterwards. You may also like to invite children to bring their own little soft toys to practice with. I also use the monkey to model the practice of Mindful sitting – and place him in my lap, with his legs crossed and his paws resting in his lap for the Meditation practice.

DELIVERY OF SESSION

MINDFUL MOVEMENT / RITUAL 1

Music: 'Air Concerto: Orchestral Suite No. 3' by Bach.

Introduce a 'Mindful Pause', beginning the session with this practice.

"Stand in your space. Create a strong base with your feet and legs to hold your body. Let your back make a strong, straight shape … and let your head feel light … like it is a balloon floating on a string … Take a big, deep breath and let your hands float up to come together in a point above your head. As you breathe out, let your hands slide down, and let one rest on your heart and the other on your tummy. Softly, quietly, say to yourself: 'Thank you body … I will practise noticing what is kind for you now.' Then, let your hands give you a big hug."

Now flow to the practice below.

MINDFUL MOVEMENT / RITUAL 2

"Now, take another big, deep breath and let your hands float up to come together in a point above your head."

1 "As you breathe out, let your hands slide down, and pause in front of **your forehead**: breathe gently and notice **kind thoughts**."

2 "Take another big, deep breath ... and as you breathe out, let your hands slide down to pause in front of **your mouth**: breathe gently and notice **kind words**."

3 "Take another big, deep breath ... and as you breathe out, let your hands slide down to pause in front of **your heart**: breathe gently and notice **kind feelings** ... for yourself, others and the world."

Introduction for students

Share the following in your own words:

"In the last session, we noticed how important it is to pause and slow down."

"When we pause there is space for good choices. Today, we will notice how we can use this space to notice our breathing, and let it calm down and help our brain to work better."

SHARING CIRCLE

Pass the Speaking Stick to a volunteer for each answer.

Q. Ask children what their body is doing to take very good care of them... right now?

A. It is doing lots of things ... all at once ... breathing, keeping the heart beating ... moving blood to feed goodness to all our cells ... digesting breakfast/morning tea/lunch .... Breathing keeps us alive.

Q. Ask which part of the body does all the thinking?

A. The brain! (Explain how it has three parts and guide children to point to these parts as you are talking).

- *There is a very fast part at the back, which keeps us alive, and helps us move very quickly **like a lizard**.*
- *There's a part in the middle that deals with all our feelings. It is lively **like a monkey**.*
- *There's a shape at the front, which does all our noticing and thinking, **like a tall, wise giraffe**.*

When we slow down, calm down and make a choice to notice our breathing and let it be slow and gentle, our brain works better.

When we breathe very quickly, we do not completely fill our lungs and we do not take enough air and oxygen to feed our cells and our brain. (Show an image of one cell: we have 50 trillion inside!). Our heart likes it when we slow down and take in some gentle, deep breaths too!.

(Partially inflate the balloon to demonstrate the little breaths we sometimes take. Then inflate the balloon completely to show how big our lungs can be when we lift our head, straighten our spine and give our chest space to take in lots of air as we breathe in).

ACTIVITY

Organise children into a circle. Introduce the toy monkey and explain how at times, our mind is just like a very busy, noisy monkey – rushing here and there, getting very excited and sometimes worrying and getting cross. When our mind is like a monkey for too long, it makes it very hard for the poor 'giraffe' part of the brain to clearly notice, think and make good choices. Then unhelpful messages can travel to the 'lizard' part of the brain, which means the body gets tight, stiff and fidgety.

Ask children to hold the fabric with their hands. Remind children that if they all notice everyone's hands moving together, it might be possible to keep the monkey on the fabric. Share the practice of breathing quickly, with the hands creating fast waves to bounce the monkey (expect lots of laughs!).

When the time is right, indicate this practice will stop now! Ask children to pause and put down the fabric. Ask them to place one hand on their heart, and one on their tummy, and notice what the body is feeling inside?

Practise 'Balloon Man Movement'.

Invite children to return to sitting together again and holding the fabric. Explain that the practice is now to help monkey calm down and return his body and mind to balance! Encourage children to synchronise their breathing, and let their hands follow the breath … rising slowly upwards with the in breath… and floating slowly down with the out breath. Share 10 connected slow breaths.

Ask children to check in to their own bodies again, and notice what inner state is there now?

Remove the monkey from the centre. You might like to let the children take it in turns to calm monkey down on their tummy for Meditation practices.

MINDFUL MOVEMENT

Practising being aware of breath with music

Music: 'Air Concerto: Orchestral Suite No. 3' by Bach.

'Balloon Man Practice'

1 "Stand with your feet spaced evenly under your hips … and your knees slightly bent. Let your spine be a strong, straight shape."

2 "Take in a deep, full breath … and let your arms float up above your head …"

3 "As you breathe out … let your head and body drop and sink down, as all the breath leaves your body. Now, breathe in, and pretend that a flow of air is coming up through the base of your feet, travelling up your legs and into your body, so your whole body feels like a 'balloon man', just like the ones you see along the road sometimes. Feel yourself getting bigger and bigger … until

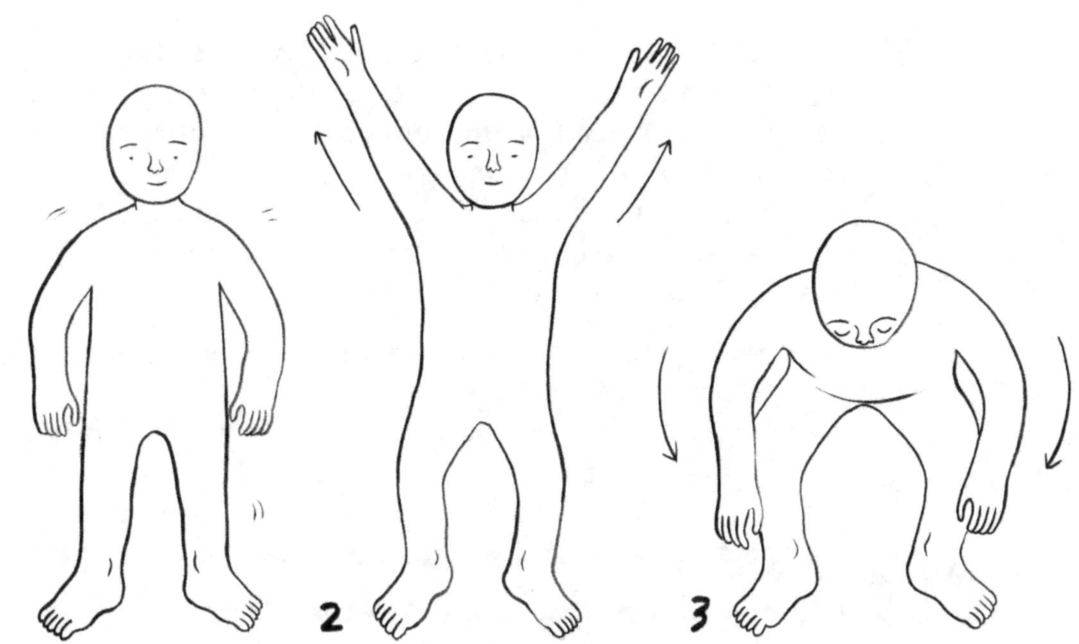

your arms are above your head again. Now, breathing out through the mouth ... let your head and body drop and sink down again."

"Repeat the movements ... and notice how these movements feel like slow, long, gentle 'waves' of air moving up and down, in and out through your whole body."

Flow quietly and slowly to your place on the floor and invite children to take off their shoes.

QUIET INNER AWARENESS/MINDFUL MEDITATION

Lying down practice

(If you wish, you can place the toy monkey on the tummy of a child).

"Stand in your quiet space and let your body find its way down to the floor ... letting it lie down on your back. Let your body feel like it is becoming a 'sea anemone' ... As you breathe in, **let your arms and legs float up in the air** ... and as you breathe out ... let them slowly, gently float back down to the floor ... just like they are moving in water ... Breathing in, and floating your arms and legs up in the air ... Breathing out ... and floating them back down to the floor ... Floating up ... and floating down." (Repeat four or more times).

"Now, **letting your feet and legs, and your hands and arms come to rest on the floor** ... Let's notice your feet now, as they lie on the floor. **Letting your feet move with the breath** ... as you breathe in opening your toes wide, ... and as you breathe out, letting them become soft and loose ... Moving your toes with the breath – tight and stiff ... then soft and loose ..." (Repeat four or more times).

"**Now, letting your hands move with the breath** ... Breathing in ... and opening your fingers wide like a star ... and breathing out ... allowing your hands to soften and letting your fingers roll into a gentle shape ... Opening wide ... and closing ... opening ... and closing ... **And now, let your hands and arms become totally quiet** ... totally still."

"**Letting your head move with the breath now, softly and gently** ... breathing in, rolling it over to one side ... and,

breathing out, letting it roll back to the middle ... Breathing
in to the other side ... and out to the centre ... Breathing
in to the other side ... and back to the centre." (Repeat
three times).

"**Now, just letting your whole body deeply rest** ... even your
eyes ... letting your eyes close down ... Can you notice the
only thing that is moving now ... is the gentle, soft, easy
waves of the breath? ... Rolling up ... and rolling down
through the body ... rolling up ... and down ... up ... and down"

Children spend a few moments in stillness and silence to fully
experience what they are feeling now.

"Feel the breath slowly deepening now ... and slowly
'wake up' your body with some stretching ... with slow, big
stretches through your arms and legs ... and then you might
like to roll over and lie on your side for a while ... until you are
ready to slowly return to sitting up."

MINDFUL MOVEMENT / RITUAL 3

A 'Mindful Farewell' for the session

Invite everyone to return to a cross-legged sitting position.

"Bring your hands to press together (with palms facing in
a 'prayer position') in a tight shape in front of your heart.
Breathe in ... and as you slowly breathe out ... let your hands
change into a soft shape, with all your fingers softening
to create a soft space inside, just like the shape of a
cocoon. Inside a cocoon, a butterfly is forming ... just like
the beautiful changes inside us when we pause and make
kind choices."

"**Hold your kind 'cocoon' hands in front of your heart.**
Breathe in ... and as you breathe out, **bow in respect and
kindness for yourself** ... Then, breathe in ... and breathe out
... and **bow with respect and kindness for others** ... Lastly,
breathe in ... and breathe out, and **bow with respect and
kindness for nature and the world**."

"Now, let your 'butterfly' hands open ... and smile ... sharing
your beautiful smile with everyone ... and wave or twinkle
all your fingers to spread your kindness to every person in
the group."

SESSION 6
The 'Just Right' choice!

TEACHER PREPARATION

RESOURCES

- Speaking Stick
- **3 Bowls:** one big, one average, one small
- **Story:** 'Goldilocks and the Three Bears' by Robert Southey
- **Music:** 'Canon in D' by Pachelbel for the Mindful Movement Ritual Opening and 'Happy' by Pharrell Williams for the Activity Movement

FOCUS WORDS

happiness
calm
comfortable

CHARACTER STRENGTHS

Perspective (understanding), self-control (self-care, awareness), fairness

LEARNING GOAL

To notice the 'just right' choices for your body and brain

The aim of this program is to help children 'befriend' themselves – to respect and value their body and mind and discover ways to learn how to take good care of it.

When we learn to settle, centre and connect the body back to balance, the brain follows.

DELIVERY OF SESSION

MINDFUL MOVEMENT / RITUAL 1

Music: 'Rainforest Environment' by Ken Davis.

Introduce a 'Mindful Pause', beginning the session with this practice.

"Stand in your space. Create a strong base with your feet and legs to hold your body … Let your back make a strong, straight shape … and let your head feel light … like it is a balloon floating on a string … Take a big, deep breath and let your hands float up to come together in a point above your head. As you breathe out, let your hands slide down, and let one rest on your heart and the other on your tummy. Softly, quietly, say to yourself: 'Thank you body … I will practise noticing what is kind for you now.' Then, let your hands give you a big hug."

Now flow to the practice below.

MINDFUL MOVEMENT / RITUAL 2

"Now, take another big, deep breath and let your hands float up to come together in a point above your head."

1 "As you breathe out, let your hands slide down, and pause in front of **your forehead**: breathe gently and notice **kind thoughts**."

2 "Take another big, deep breath … and as you breathe out, let your hands slide down to pause in front of **your mouth**: breathe gently and notice **kind words**."

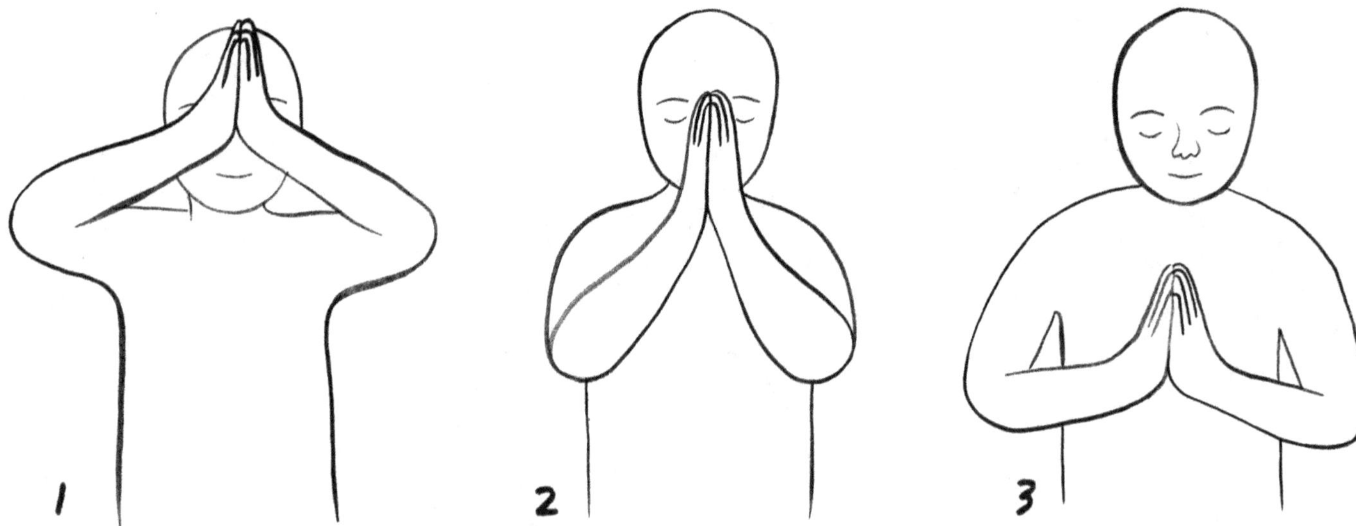

3 "Take another big, deep breath ... and as you breathe out, let your hands slide down to pause in front of **your heart**: breathe gently and notice **kind feelings** ... for yourself, others and the world."

Share the following in your own words:

"Every day and every moment, there are lots of choices we can make. We are constantly choosing ... what we will eat, wear, play and do next."

"When we slow down and calm down, we can remember the happy, kind choices we can make for ourselves and others."

SHARING CIRCLE

Share the story of 'Goldilocks and the Three Bears'. As you share the story, use the props of the three bowls.

Pass the Speaking Stick to a volunteer for each answer.

Q. What kind of choices did Goldilocks make?

A. She made good choices for herself ... with the chairs, bowls of porridge and the beds.

Q. Did she choose to notice what the three bears would think?

A. She did not think about what the bears would think about helping herself to all their things!

"Mindfulness practices, like slowing down, pausing and choosing carefully, help us to make good choices – for us, others and the world."

"When we notice what makes us feel happy, calm and just right, our brains work better to make good choices for others."

"When we make good choices for ourselves, and we feel calm and happy, we can better notice the kind choices to make for other people."

ACTIVITY

Music: 'Happy' by Pharrell Williams.

"Let's discover the 'Just Right' movements our body would like to make with this song."

"As we move, let's notice the moves our happy body would like to make." (Give one suggestion at a time, so children can notice moving each part of the body).

- Which moves would our happy feet like to do?
- How would our happy legs like to move?
- How would our happy hands and arms like to move?
- What shape would your happy spine like to be in, with your happy shoulders and your happy head?
- What happy shapes would your whole body like to make?

Take a moment after the movement to catch your breath … and let your body calm down.

QUIET INNER AWARENESS/MINDFUL MEDITATION

Sitting practice

"Allow your **body to settle into a quiet place** … **and space, sitting still with your legs crossed**. This is a time for you to notice and discover what is 'just right' for all the different parts of your body."

"**Let's start with your feet** … and let them settle into the best spot on the floor to rest … Then you can notice your legs … and making any little movements that help your feet to feel comfy … Letting your feet and legs settle into a 'triangle shape' … feeling 'Just Right' through your feet and legs."

"**As you gently notice your own body** ... let your eyes rest ... just letting them close gently down ... so that you can notice the feelings in your body better."

"**Now we can notice how our back feels** ... just letting it sway a little, just a little bit, from one side ... to the other side ... Letting it sway to one side with the in-breath ... and to the other side with the out-breath ... from side ... to side ... swaying across the middle point. Then, letting your spine find its own way back to the middle ... finding its own 'Just Right' spot ... to rest, right in the middle of your body."

"**Now we can notice our hands** ... let them open (palms facing up) ... and close (palms facing down) ... Opening with the in-breath ... and closing with the out-breath (Repeat three times) ... **Letting your hands tell you now the 'Just Right' way in which they would like to rest** ... and just letting your hands become still."

"**Notice your shoulders now** ... breathe in and feeling your shoulders rise up and tighten... and breathing out ... letting them drop down to feel loose ... and soft." (Repeat three times).

"**Now notice your head** ... let it feel light ... and soft ... and float over your body ... rocking from front ... to back ... front ... to back ... and then softly and gently, from side ... to side ... side ... to side ... until your head finds its own gentle resting space right over the middle of your body ... a resting place for your head to be still and quiet."

"**Noticing your whole body now** ... feeling calm, settled and still ... and feeling **'Just Right'** all over ..."

Children spend a few moments in stillness and silence to fully experience what they are feeling now.

"When you are ready ... take some slow, deep breaths ... bring your attention back to the room ... and do some big stretches through your arms and legs."

A 'Mindful Farewell' for the session

Invite everyone to return to a cross-legged sitting position.

"Bring your hands to press together (with palms facing in a 'prayer position') in a tight shape in front of your heart. Breathe in … and as you slowly breathe out … let your hands change into a soft shape, with all your fingers softening to create a soft space inside, just like the shape of a cocoon. Inside a cocoon, a butterfly is forming … just like the beautiful changes inside us when we pause and make kind choices."

"**Hold your kind 'cocoon' hands in front of your heart.** Breathe in … and as you breathe out, **bow in respect and kindness for yourself** … Then, breathe in … and breathe out … and **bow with respect and kindness for others** … Lastly, breathe in … and breathe out, and **bow with respect and kindness for nature and the world**."

"Now, let your 'butterfly' hands open … and smile … sharing your beautiful smile with everyone … and wave or twinkle all your fingers to spread your kindness to every person in the group."

PART THREE

Noticing the senses

"Curiosity is as much the parent of attention, as attention is of memory." — RICHARD WHATELY

Character Strengths

- Curiosity
- Open-Mindedness
- Appreciation of Beauty and Excellence
- Humour and Playfulness

The saying 'come to your senses' reminds us to wake up to a tangible reality that is accessible now. The realm of the senses offers a diverse palette of possibilities and opportunities to effortlessly engage children. As they become immersed in tangible experiences, children become settled and centred.

Connection to the senses is not limited to the basic five starting points of sight, smell, hearing, taste and touch. Awareness can be extended to the senses of balance, movement, proprioception, temperature, gut sense, heart sense and the sense of feeling and experiencing external and internal sensations. You may like to explore some of these with the children in your care.

Part 3 refines the skills of noticing through the entry points of the senses. Attention to the senses provides an effective 'anchor point' for the mind. Focus on the senses effectively connects to all learning styles and engages children with ease and joy. It is a delight to observe children discovering the 'extraordinary in the ordinary' – to perceive beyond superficial noticing, experiencing deeper levels of awareness as focus is sustained.

Session 7 supports the character strengths of curiosity, appreciation of beauty and excellence and humour and playfulness, through active listening and appreciation of sounds. These practices develop the skills of deep focus and discernment.

Session 8 supports the same strengths as Session 7. Connection to sight brings countless possibilities and opportunities for engagement and personal discoveries. It also presents a wonderful opportunity for connection to the wonders of the natural world.

Session 9 introduces the senses of touch and feeling. Once again, the character strength of curiosity is embraced, along with open-mindedness. Activities encourage children to experience outer and inner awareness. Practising noticing leads to knowing in the present moment and over time the skill of inner-knowing is cultivated.

Tuning into sound

TEACHER PREPARATION

RESOURCES

- Speaking Stick
- Singing bowl/chimes/triangle
- **Music:** 'The Moonlight Sonata', Piano Sonata #14 in C Sharp, Beethoven for the Mindful Movement Ritual Greeting and 'Carnival of the Animals' by Saint-Saëns for the Activity

LEARNING GOAL

To achieve connection and engagement with sounds

FOCUS WORDS

curiosity
purpose
senses
hearing
listening
volume – loud, soft

CHARACTER STRENGTHS

Curiosity, appreciation of beauty and excellence, humour and playfulness

TIPS

Become familiar with the music before the session.

Notice how quickly and effortlessly music connects to you, and observe how quickly it can change the 'state' that you are in.

Listen to some of the different sections of 'Carnival of the Animals' and see if you can identify the animals yourself. Decide how you want to draw out discussion with the children.

Awareness is like a multi-faceted diamond. In this program, we are connecting to and exploring many different 'jewels'. Activities are designed to direct, connect and maintain children's attention, to enable them to make deep, personal discoveries and build strong neural networks in the brain. Fun-filled ways to deepen focus and concentration and bring about settled, calm states in the body and mind.

DELIVERY OF SESSION

MINDFUL MOVEMENT / RITUAL 1

Music: 'The Moonlight Sonata', Piano Sonata #14 in C Sharp, Beethoven.

Introduce a 'Mindful Pause', beginning the session with this practice.

"Stand in your space. Create a strong base with your feet and legs to hold your body. Let your back make a strong, straight shape … and let your head feel light … like it is a balloon floating on a string … Take a big, deep breath and let your hands float up to come together in a point above your head. As you breathe out, let your hands slide down, and let one rest on your heart and the other on your tummy. Softly, quietly, say to yourself: 'Thank you body … I will practise noticing what is kind for you now.' Then, let your hands give you a big hug."

Now flow to the practice below.

MINDFUL MOVEMENT / RITUAL 2

"Now, take another big, deep breath and let your hands float up to come together in a point above your head."

1 "As you breathe out, let your hands slide down, and pause in front of **your forehead**: breathe gently and notice **kind thoughts**."

2 "Take another big, deep breath … and as you breathe out, let your hands slide down to pause in front of **your mouth**: breathe gently and notice **kind words**."

3 "Take another big, deep breath … and as you breathe out, let your hands slide down to pause in front of **your heart**: breathe gently and notice **kind feelings** … for yourself, others and the world."

Share the following in your own words:

"Today we are going to notice sounds. We can be curious about noticing sounds and how they make us feel."

"When we pause, and become calm and still, we can notice really well, just like a calm, tall giraffe that can see and hear everything!"

SHARING CIRCLE

Pass the Speaking Stick to a volunteer for each answer.

Q. What is the difference between 'hearing' and 'listening'?

*A. When we hear things, we are not always giving them our full attention. When we mindfully listen, we are **noticing on purpose** (we are making a decision to notice).*

Q. Why do you think Mindful listening is important?

A. Sounds take important messages to the brain. Life is full of sounds, some of which we need to notice and others that we don't. We have to notice certain sounds in order to be safe. For example, noticing the sound of a kettle boiling and realising it is hot; noticing someone is crying, and needs help and comfort; noticing sounds in the car such as sirens from ambulances or the fire brigade. There are also all kinds of sounds that give us pleasure and make us feel happy.

Q. What are your favourite sounds? What do you really like to listen to?

A. Use prompts if necessary. For example, man-made sounds – TV, music, aeroplanes, machines, clocks; sounds of people singing, talking and laughing; and sounds from nature – wind, rain, birds, dogs, cats and frogs.

ACTIVITY

Play 'Elephant', 'Lion' and then 'Swan' from 'Carnival of the Animals'. Ask children to identify the animal they think each piece of music suggests. Prompt students to describe what they noticed.

Flow into 'Mindful Movement' – how does their body want to move with the 'Elephant' music, the 'Lion' music and finally the 'Swan' music? In a natural way, invite the character strengths of humour and playfulness into this practice.

Play the 'Swan' music and invite children to flow into their quiet space.

QUIET INNER AWARENESS/MINDFUL MEDITATION

Sitting practice

"Notice your body settling down into its special shape, to be still and quiet. For this practice, your body might like to choose a sitting shape … with your legs crossed, and your back straight and strong … This is another chance to practice growing a calm body and wise mind."

"Perhaps your body might feel like a tall, calm, wise giraffe … with a long, long neck … and big, alert, soft ears … Being very still … noticing **everything** … What **sounds** can you notice? … See if you can hear sounds outside … Perhaps you can hear **loud sounds**: like cars, machines, or even an aeroplane flying overhead … Maybe you can hear more gentle sounds … like the wind … or the rain … perhaps birds singing … or insects buzzing …"

"Now … shift your noticing … and **bring it back to listen to sounds in the room** … Perhaps you can hear a clock ticking … a fan whirring … or a light buzzing …?"

"Let's notice this next sound … **(Use chimes, a singing bowl or triangle)** …Can you notice the sound vibrating … and moving through the space … becoming softer … and softer?"

"And now … letting your attention come home to you … home to your breath … so you can notice the gentle, soft sound of your own breath … As you are breathing, realising that there is nothing that you have to change … nothing you have to control ... Just sitting quietly and still ... noticing your breathing becoming softer ... and softer ... slowing down ... and settling with your body."

Children spend a few moments in stillness and silence to fully experience what they are feeling now.

"When you are ready ... Take some slow, deep breaths ... And bring your attention back ... and have some big stretches through your arms and legs."

MINDFUL MOVEMENT / RITUAL 3

A 'Mindful Farewell' for the session

Invite everyone to return to a cross-legged sitting position.

"Bring your hands to press together (with palms facing in a 'prayer position') in a tight shape in front of your heart. Breathe in ... and as you slowly breathe out ... let your hands change into a soft shape, with all your fingers softening to create a soft space inside, just like the shape of a cocoon. Inside a cocoon, a butterfly is forming ... just like the beautiful changes inside us when we pause and make kind choices."

"**Hold your kind 'cocoon' hands in front of your heart**. Breathe in ... and as you breathe out, **bow in respect and kindness for yourself** ... Then, breathe in ... and breathe out ... and **bow with respect and kindness for others** ... Lastly, breathe in ... and breathe out, and **bow with respect and kindness for nature and the world**."

"Now, let your 'butterfly' hands open ... and smile ... sharing your beautiful smile with everyone ... and wave or twinkle all your fingers to spread your kindness to every person in the group."

Seeing what's extraordinary

TEACHER PREPARATION

RESOURCES

- Speaking Stick
- A small torch/flashlight
- **Selection of natural objects:** A range of feathers, leaves, wood, grasses, seed pods, flowers, spices, shells, rocks etc.
- **Books:** Your choice: 'Where's Wally?' by Martin Handford; 'Wild About Shapes' by Jeremie Fischer; Escher artwork books; 'Belonging' & other books by Jeannie Baker; or 'Spot the Difference' cartoons
- **Music:** 'Gymnopédies No. 1. Lent et Douloureux' by Erik Satie for the Mindful Movement Ritual Greeting and Mindful Movement

FOCUS WORDS

curiosity   details
purpose   patterns
look   shapes
see

CHARACTER STRENGTHS

Curiosity, appreciation of beauty and excellence, humour and playfulness

LEARNING GOAL

To achieve connection and engagement with sight and notice the extraordinary in the ordinary

TIPS

To prepare for this session, spend some time looking at your choice of visuals (books, cartoons and specimens). Bring your awareness to the difference between just *vaguely looking* at the examples and then *clearly seeing* with full Mindful attention and a sense of purpose. You can then direct students' attention to things that they might miss.

Prepare displays of natural visual specimens in categories, so that you can arrange them around the room. Divide children into groups of 3 to 4, so they can move from one display to another.

There is a wonderful quote by Robertson Davies: "The eye sees only what the mind is prepared to comprehend". Also, this great quote comes from India: "When a pick pocket sees a saint, all he sees are his pockets".

The overarching aim of this program is to lead children on a journey of discovery. In Session 7, the focus was to connect to sounds and this session is designed to help children enjoy looking more deeply, with a greater sense of curiosity and wonder. (The way scientists look at things!).

DELIVERY OF SESSION

MINDFUL MOVEMENT / RITUAL 1

Music: 'Gymnopédies No. 1. Lent et Douloureux' by Erik Satie.

Introduce a 'Mindful pause' to begin the session with this practice.

"Stand in your space. Create a strong base with your feet and legs to hold your body ... Let your back make a strong, straight shape ... and let your head feel light ... like it is a balloon floating on a string ... Take a big, deep breath and let your hands float up to come together in a point above your head. As you breathe out, let your hands slide down, and let one rest on your heart and the other on your tummy. Softly, quietly, say to yourself: 'Thank you body ... I will practise noticing what is kind for you now.' Then, let your hands give you a big hug."

Now flow to the practice below.

MINDFUL MOVEMENT / RITUAL 2

"Now, take another big, deep breath and let your hands float up to come together in a point above your head."

1 "As you breathe out, let your hands slide down, and pause in front of **your forehead**: breathe gently and notice **kind thoughts**."

2 "Take another big, deep breath ... and as you breathe out, let your hands slide down to pause in front of **your mouth**: breathe gently and notice **kind words**."

3 "Take another big, deep breath ... and as you breathe out, let your hands slide down to pause in front of **your heart**: breathe gently and notice **kind feelings** ... for yourself, others and the world."

Share the following in your own words:

"In the last Mindfulness session, we practised noticing sounds with our ears."

"Today we will practise noticing with our eyes, so that we can see clearly. When we slow down and become still, our eyes work better. Eyes help us to see amazing things – like all the tiny patterns in a piece of wood, the beautiful shapes inside a shell and the wonderful tiny details in the middle of a flower."

SHARING CIRCLE

Pass the Speaking Stick to a volunteer for each answer.

Q. What is the difference between 'looking' and 'seeing'?

A. Just like hearing and listening, when we really pay attention on purpose, we notice more and what we are looking at becomes much more interesting. When we pause, become curious and see clearly, more information gets to our brain.

"Let's tune our eyes in now, to notice how every feather has a different flight path and makes different shapes as it floats down to the floor." (Ask children to take turns holding a feather high above their heads and see how differently they float down to the floor.)

Show examples of specimens from nature and books. Explain that if we do not pause and really notice, we miss things and the brain does not get all the information.

MINDFUL MOVEMENT

Music: 'Gymnopédies No. 1. Lent et Douloureux' by Erik Satie.

1 "Choose a space for your body to curl up in a kneeling shape, with your body rolled over your legs (just like a small seed). Make a resting place for your eyes with your hands: make two soft 'bowl shapes' with your hands and place them on your closed eyes inside each hand. Pause … noticing the warmth of your wonderful hands spreading all through your eyelids … and into your eyes …" (30 seconds)

2 "Slowly let your back return to being straight ... and blink your eyes ... almost like your eyelids are butterfly wings, fluttering over your eyes ..."

3 "Now, change your shape ... just like you are a little seed becoming a tiny seedling ... by growing ... and growing ... into a tall person again."

4 "Let your body stretch ... like your arms are shoots ... reaching up towards the sun ... Feeling calm ... fresh ... and ready to notice lots of wonderful things with your Mindful eyes."

ACTIVITY

Remind children that when we pause and become quiet and still, we focus our attention really well. We turn on our sharp, bright light of awareness (like the torch that we used in Session 1).

Show children a selection of natural specimens, inviting them to really take notice and see what is amazing, fascinating and extraordinary when they notice very carefully.

Ask the children to share what shapes, textures, patterns and tiny details they can notice. Invite everyone to share their unique discoveries.

Now flow to the practice below.

QUIET INNER AWARENESS/MINDFUL MEDITATION

Sitting and lying down practice

"**Notice your body moving down into its special shape, to be still and quiet**. For this practice, **your body might like to choose a sitting shape again** ... with your legs crossed, and your back straight and strong ... another chance to practise growing a calm, wise mind."

"**Keeping your eyes open**, let's notice what you can see outside now, through the door or window ... **Can you see things changing as you watch?**" (e.g. clouds passing by, wind moving trees and leaves, people moving, cars coming and going)."

"What shapes can you see? ... What colours can you see?"

"**Now, let's shift our attention so that we can take notice inside** ... noticing what we can see in this room ... noticing all the shapes and colours ... Is anything changing in the room?"

"**Then, gently bring your noticing home to your beautiful body** ... noticing the colours and shapes of your feet ... and legs ... hands ... and arms ... Your body ... and the clothes that you are wearing ... socks, leggings, pants, dress, t-shirt, jumper ..."

"**Now let your body change shape** ... resting into a lying down shape ... and let your curious eyes rest in one spot ... looking at the ceiling ... noticing what you can see ..."

"**Now slowly, softly, gently ... let your eyes close ... down** ... When your eyes are shut ... be curious to **notice what you can see inside with your imagination** ... 'See your breath' ... like a beautiful mist of soft colour ... Choose your favourite: white or silver ... soft blue or pink or green ... See it flowing in and out through your nose ... spreading kindness through your face ... all through your head ... and into your body."

Children spend a few moments in stillness and silence to fully experience what they are now feeling.

"When you are ready, take some slow, deep breaths ... Bring your attention back ... and do some big stretches through your arms and legs."

MINDFUL MOVEMENT / RITUAL 3

A 'Mindful Farewell' for the session

Invite everyone to return to a cross-legged sitting position.

"Bring your hands to press together (with palms facing in a 'prayer position') in a tight shape in front of your heart. Breathe in ... and as you slowly breathe out ... let your hands change into a soft shape, with all your fingers softening to create a soft space inside, just like the shape of a cocoon. Inside a cocoon, a butterfly is forming ... just like the beautiful changes inside us when we pause and make kind choices."

"**Hold your kind 'cocoon' hands in front of your heart**. Breathe in ... and as you breathe out, **bow in respect and kindness for yourself** ... Then, breathe in ... and breathe out ... and **bow with respect and kindness for others** ... Lastly, breathe in ... and breathe out, and **bow with respect and kindness for nature and the world**."

"Now, let your 'butterfly' hands open ... and smile ... sharing your beautiful smile with everyone ... and wave or twinkle all your fingers to spread your kindness to every person in the group."

Touch – outside and inside

TEACHER PREPARATION

RESOURCES

- Speaking Stick
- Thin socks/pieces of thin, soft fabric
- Rubber bands
- **Mystery objects:** A variety of soft or hard little 'mystery' objects to place inside the socks/material. For example: sponges, cotton balls, rubber bands, cotton reels, little plastic toys, tiny bottles/jars, spoons, buttons and seed pods
- **Music:** 'Daintree Rainforest' by Ken Davis

FOCUS WORDS

hard	bumpy
soft	spiky
smooth	spongy
jagged	dry and moist

CHARACTER STRENGTHS

Curiosity, open-mindedness

LEARNING GOAL

To wake up our hands and feelings: outside our body and inside

TIPS

Take opportunities to notice the sense of touch. Practice pausing to notice the touch of air on skin, clothes against your body, and how feeling different surfaces and textures makes you more aware of feelings and sensations through your whole body.

Find everyday opportunities to take your awareness inside the body to notice with kindness what internal states the body is in, and ways to return it to balance and harmony (e.g. in the shower, sitting down with a cup of tea, or before bed).

The sense of touch is an intimate one. This session leads children on a playful journey to become curious about what they can notice with their hands, extending this sense of curiosity to notice, without judging, different feelings and sensations inside their own body.

Mindfulness practices bring wonderful opportunities to notice feelings inside, which may often be uncomfortable (tight, stiff, hard, blocked), and to discover simple, kind ways to soothe and calm these feelings (with the breath, stretching, movement and stillness).

DELIVERY OF SESSION

Music: 'Daintree Rainforest' by Ken Davis.

Invite children to pause, stand still and just listen to this music for about 60 seconds, using their sense of curiosity to notice all the sounds of nature they can hear. Then turn down the volume of the music and proceed with the Mindful Movement Ritual to start the session.

MINDFUL MOVEMENT / RITUAL 1

Music: 'Daintree Rainforest' by Ken Davis.

Introduce a 'Mindful Pause', beginning the session with this practice.

"Stand in your space. Create a strong base with your feet and legs to hold your body. Let your back make a strong, straight shape … and let your head feel light … like it is a balloon floating on a string … Take a big, deep breath and let your hands float up to come together in a point above your head. As you breathe out, let your hands slide down, and let one rest on your heart and the other on your tummy. Softly, quietly, say to yourself: 'Thank you body … I will practise noticing what is kind for you now.' Then, let your hands give you a big hug."

Now flow to the practice below.

MINDFUL MOVEMENT / RITUAL 2

"Now, take another big, deep breath and let your hands float up to come together in a point above your head."

1 "As you breathe out, let your hands slide down, and pause in front of **your forehead**: breathe gently and notice **kind thoughts**."

2 "Take another big, deep breath … and as you breathe out, let your hands slide down to pause in front of **your mouth**: breathe gently and notice **kind words**."

3 "Take another big, deep breath … and as you breathe out, let your hands slide down to pause in front of **your heart**: breathe gently and notice **kind feelings** … for yourself, others and the world."

Introduction for students

Share the following in your own words:

"Our focus today is to notice what we can feel and touch."

"We can notice all kinds of things when we feel and touch with our hands. As we grow our Mindfulness skills, we can notice more and more things: even noticing feelings inside our bodies."

SHARING CIRCLE

Pass the Speaking Stick to a volunteer for each answer.

Q. Which parts of our body can we use to feel and touch things?

A. Hands, feet, skin all over our body. On the inside, too – mouth, chest, tummy.

Q. What do we notice when we touch things?

A. Feelings: hot/cold, smooth/rough; soft/hard; tight/loose. These feelings can feel nice or not so nice – even yucky!

Q. What are some things you love to feel?

A. Sand, pets, clothes, blankets, water and food.

Q. What are some things that you don't like to feel?

A. Too hot, too cold, gravel, sharp rocks, prickly plants and slimy things.

"Now we are going to notice feeling 'mystery parcels'. This is a quiet noticing practice, so we do not talk to anyone when we do it. Feel five 'parcels', with closed eyes, and see if you can figure out what is inside. When you have finished, keep your eyes closed and see if you can remember what they are!"

Invite feedback from children.

MINDFUL MOVEMENT

Qigong – 'Dissolving the Clouds'

Music: 'Daintree Rainforest' by Ken Davis.

1 "Let your feet find a strong space on the floor to hold you, so they are just under your hips. Let your knees bend a little and feel soft. Let your back be straight ... shoulders soft ... and let your head feel light ... as if it is floating over your body."

2 "Let your hands and arms be loose and soft ... Cross them in front of the body ... and as you take a deep breath in ..."

3 "Let your hands float up as if they were carried up by the breath ... until they rise above your head."

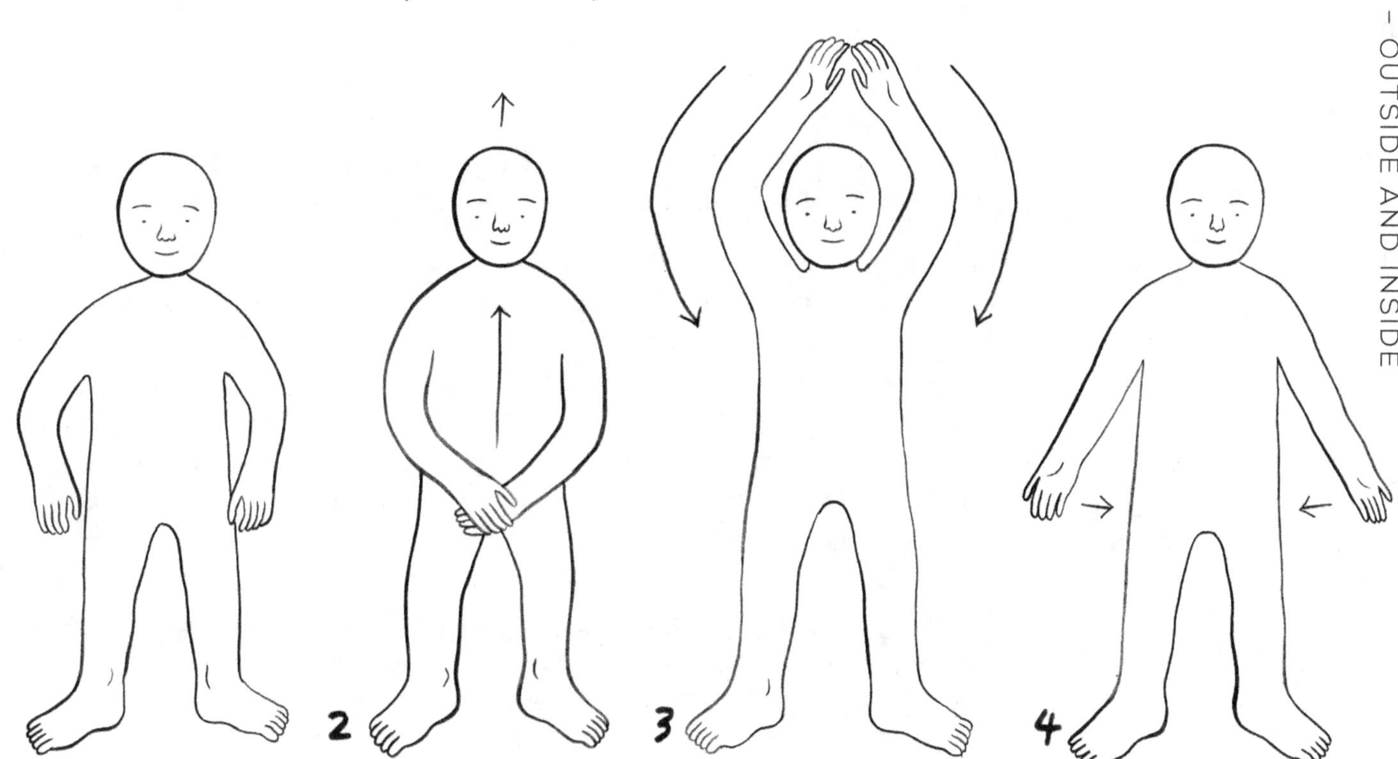

4 "Then, as you breathe out … let them float out … just like they are clearing a beautiful space all around you … and float down, making a circle shape beside you until they come to rest by your body."

(Repeat this movement five times).

Now flow to the practice below.

QUIET INNER AWARENESS/MINDFUL MEDITATION

Sitting and lying down practice

"**Notice your body settle down into its special shape, to be still and quiet**. To begin this practice, your body might like to choose a sitting shape again, with your legs crossed, and your back straight and strong … another chance to practice growing a calm body and wise mind."

"In the activity we just shared, we noticed feeling shapes in the mystery parcels with our hands … now we are going to notice feelings inside our body."

"**Let's start by noticing our hands … and feel them changing shape**, just like a beautiful flower in a garden … opening and closing its petals. Breathing in … and letting your fingers open really wide … and then, gently breathing out … allowing your fingers to enjoy softening, letting go … and curling back into a soft, round shape like a sponge … Opening wide … and then letting go … Moving open … and closed … with the breath. Then just letting your hands rest in a soft, quiet shape …"

"**When you are ready, let your body change shape** … letting it come to rest … lying on your back on the floor … Feeling the surface of the hard floor underneath you … and noticing your soft body resting on the floor … even noticing the touch of your clothes against your skin … **Feeling your hands now** … When you breathe in feeling them float up beside you … and when you breathe out, float back down … Feeling the air moving around your hands … Now, feeling your hands slowly, gently rising up once more … then letting them float down again to choose a safe, quiet place to land on your tummy. **Letting your tummy feel soft and loose now** … so the gentle waves of the breath can roll easily through it … in

… and out … up … and down … and letting the gentle waves of the breath rock your soft hands … Letting them become softer … and softer …"

"**And as your calm, quiet hands feel like they are dozing on your tummy … notice the feeling inside your body** … inside your tummy … Feeling the gentle softness spread … all through your tummy … and up into your chest and heart … Soothing waves flowing through your body … down your legs and feet … across your shoulders and down your arms and hands … Softness spreading smoothly and easily up into your neck, face and head."

Children spend a few moments in stillness and silence to fully experience what they are feeling now.

"When you are ready … take some slow, deep breaths … Bring your attention back to the room … and enjoy some big stretches through your arms and legs."

MINDFUL MOVEMENT / RITUAL 3

A 'Mindful Farewell' for the session

Invite everyone to return to a cross-legged sitting position.

"Bring your hands to press together (with palms facing in a 'prayer position') in a tight shape in front of your heart. Breathe in … and as you slowly breathe out … let your hands change into a soft shape, with all your fingers softening to create a soft space inside, just like the shape of a cocoon. Inside a cocoon, a butterfly is forming … just like the beautiful changes inside us when we pause and make kind choices."

"**Hold your kind 'cocoon' hands in front of your heart**. Breathe in … and as you breathe out, **bow in respect and kindness for yourself** … Then, breathe in … and breathe out … and **bow with respect and kindness for others** … Lastly, breathe in … and breathe out, and **bow with respect and kindness for nature and the world**."

"Now, let your 'butterfly' hands open … and smile … sharing your beautiful smile with everyone … and wave or twinkle all your fingers to spread your kindness to every person in the group."

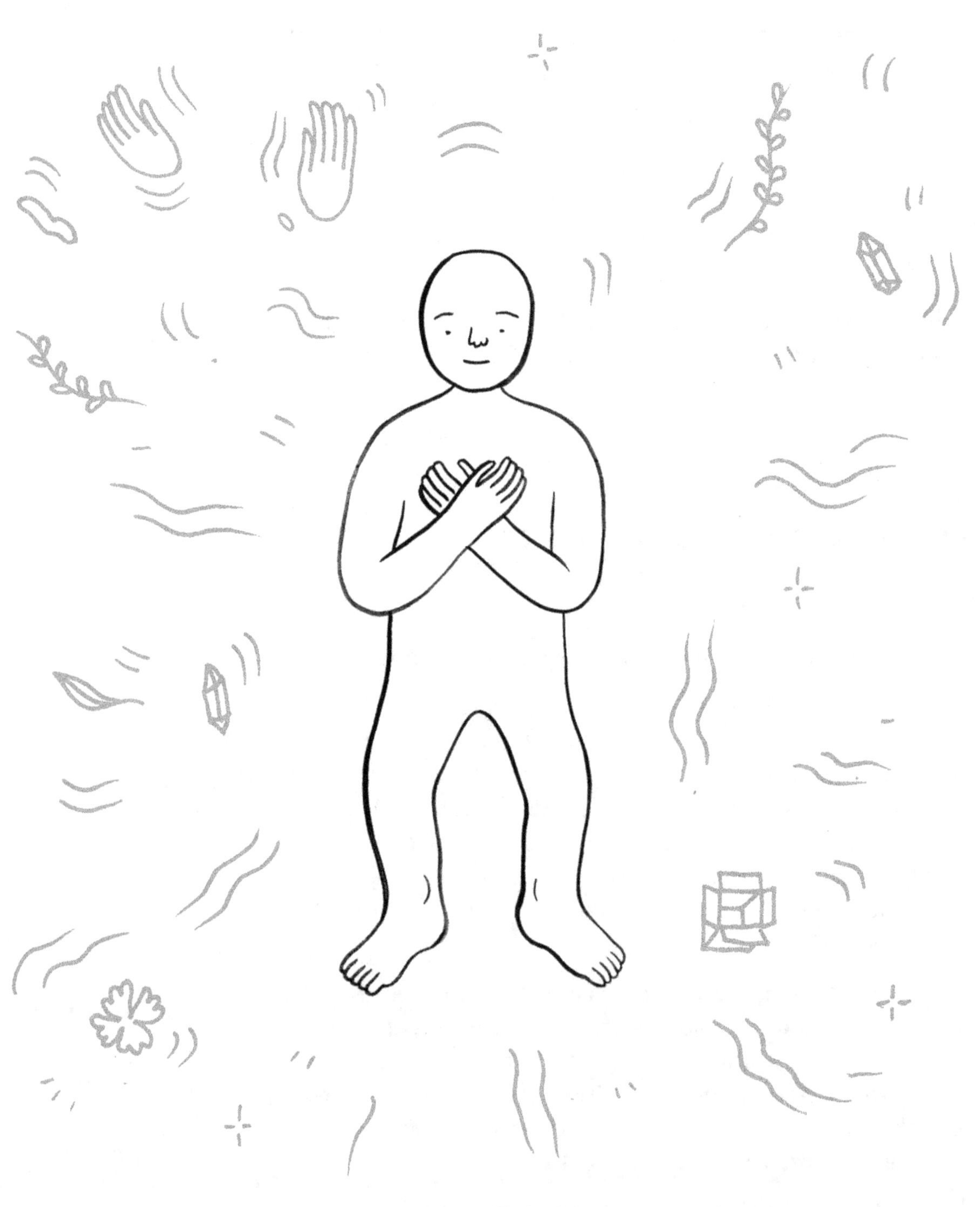

Noticing with the heart

"Wherever you go, go with all your heart." — CONFUCIUS

Character Strengths

- Curiosity
- Creativity
- Love
- Kindness
- Gratitude

- Forgiveness
- Fairness
- Teamwork
- Zest (enthusiasm)
- Perspective (wisdom)

The brain is a magnificent and very important part of the mind, but our mind extends beyond the jawline! Neuroscientist Candace Pert, author of the book 'Molecules of Emotion', reminded us that the body is our unconscious mind and the heart is the centre of this field of information and intelligence.

The main component of the parasympathetic nervous system (which signals the relaxation response) is the vagus nerve. This is a complex nerve network linking the entire body/brain function. It relays messages up to the brain, with 80% of its fibres running in this direction. Messages traveling along this nerve from the heart and the gut have a big impact on the functioning of the brain.

A compassionate development of Mindfulness embraces the heart sense. As awareness of the heart grows, so does empathy, wisdom and a host of character strengths. Love, kindness, forgiveness, gratitude, zest and perspective flow from heart-centred awareness, and are integral to this program. Cultivation of these strengths helps rewire the brain for happiness.

Session 10 focuses on the character strengths of kindness and love. The session begins with time to wonder what kindness is and remember how different parts of the body can be used to share kindness. A hands-on activity brings this contemplation to life. The theme is extended with Mindful Movements and meditation practices.

Session 11 embraces the character strength of zest (enthusiasm), as well as gratitude and perspective (wisdom). As the mind has evolved with a negativity bias to help us survive, it is important to cultivate heartfelt awareness of states of curiosity, awe, wonder and appreciation.

In the words of Albert Einstein: 'The most beautiful thing we can experience is the mysterious. It is the source of all true art and science'.

Session 12 embraces the character strengths of love, kindness and gratitude. Shared reflections and activities guide children to the awareness that peace, like happiness, is not far away. It is something that can be noticed, cultivated and experienced now, in all kinds of wonderful ways.

Nurturing kindness

TEACHER PREPARATION

RESOURCES

- Speaking Stick
- Mung beans
- Clean glass jar
- Piece of porous fabric (eg. Chux)
- Rubber bands
- Large bowl of water
- Sieve
- **Music:** 'Kodama Tree Spirit' by Jane Rutter for the Mindful Movement Ritual Greeting and 'This Little Light of Mine', Bible Songs for Children for Mindful Movement

FOCUS WORDS

heart
kindness
caring
connection

CHARACTER STRENGTHS

Kindness, love

LEARNING GOAL

To notice kindness

TIPS

Reflect on all the ways that you practise kindness to yourself, and all the kind actions and choices you make for others and the world.

Consider ways kindness can grow in the Centre and at home with the children, staff and families.

I n 2008 the UK Government published a document recommending five actions to improve personal wellbeing. Connection and giving were two of the five ways for people to be happy and well. (The others were activity, taking notice and learning).

The study showed the benefits of noticing what is kind for the body and mind (including Mindful choices of food, activity, rest), and how sharing kindness (with others, animals and nature) can lead to increased health and happiness.

DELIVERY OF SESSION

MINDFUL MOVEMENT / RITUAL 1

Music: 'Kodama Tree Spirit', by Jane Rutter.

Introduce a 'Mindful Pause', beginning the session with this practice.

"Stand in your space. Create a strong base with your feet and legs to hold your body. Let your back make a strong, straight shape … and let your head feel light … like it is a balloon floating on a string … Take a big, deep breath and let your hands float up to come together in a point above your head. As you breathe out, let your hands slide down, and let one rest on your heart and the other on your

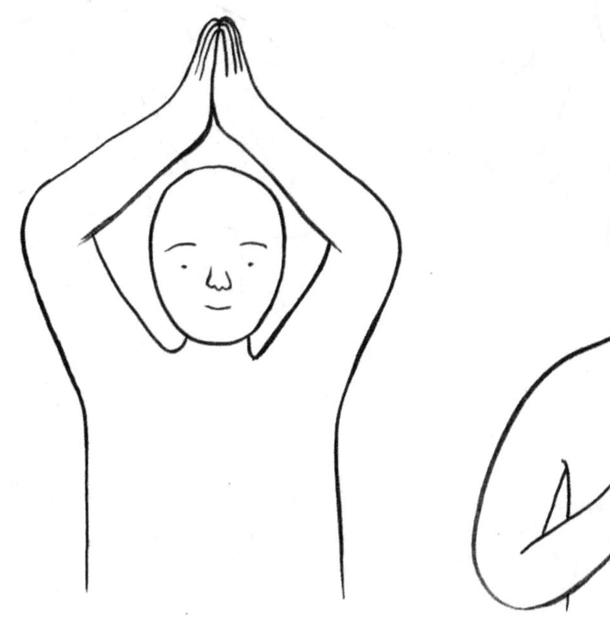

tummy. Softly, quietly, say to yourself: 'Thank you body ... I will practise noticing what is kind for you now.' Then, let your hands give you a big hug."

Now flow to the practice below.

MINDFUL MOVEMENT / RITUAL 2

"Now, take another big, deep breath and let your hands float up to come together in a point above your head."

1 "As you breathe out, let your hands slide down, and pause in front of **your forehead**: breathe gently and notice **kind thoughts**."

2 "Take another big, deep breath ... and as you breathe out, let your hands slide down to pause in front of **your mouth**: breathe gently and notice **kind words**."

3 "Take another big, deep breath ... and as you breathe out, let your hands slide down to pause in front of **your heart**: breathe gently and notice **kind feelings** ... for yourself, others and the world."

Share the following in your own words:

"Mindfulness is all about noticing. When we pause, we can notice what shape we are in, what state we are in and, most importantly, what choices we are making."

"We have taken part in many sessions about noticing how we feel and the choices we make. Now we will practise noticing with our heart – noticing what kindness is and how we can grow kind minds to feel happier and share kindness and happiness."

SHARING CIRCLE

Pass the Speaking Stick to a volunteer for each answer.

Q. What does kindness mean?

A. Caring, loving thoughts, words and actions.

Q. How can we spread the 'messages from our heart' by doing kind actions?

A. Sharing, giving, listening carefully, saying kind words and helping people.

Q. What kind things can we do with our hands?

A. Wave, pat, hug, hold hands, make things, give things, help people, help the environment: pick up rubbish, water plants, and turn off lights.

Q. What kind things can we do with our mouth?

A. Smile, say kind words and exchange kisses.

Q. What kind things can we do with our eyes?

A. Respectfully notice and pay attention so we can see what matters.

Q. What kind things can we do with our whole body?

A. Be still to pay respectful attention, turn to face people and help others.

ACTIVITY

Explain to children that kindness is something that grows with experience and practice. Every time we feel kind and do something kind, we become a kinder person. Every time we are kind, our actions remind other people to be kind.

Ask children to sit in a circle, placing a bowl of water in the middle. Give each child a mung bean and invite them, one at a time, to drop it into the water bowl. Ask them to verbalise kind things that they do – for example smiling, listening carefully, caring for people, animals and plants, helping, sharing and giving. Invite them to watch the ripples the bean makes as it enters the water. Remind children that every kind action creates ripples that touch other people's lives as well as extending into the natural world of insects, animals, plants, trees, waterways and the ocean.

Put the beans in a jar covered with water, leaving them to soak overnight. The next day, place some fabric over the top of the jar, securing this with a rubber band, and pour out all the water. Rinse the beans each day and remember to give children opportunities to watch the beans grow. After about three days the sprouted beans can be shared for lunch!

MINDFUL MOVEMENT

Music: 'This Little Light of Mine', Bible Songs for Children.

Invite children to stand in a circle, with everyone facing inwards.

1 "**Let's start with our feet** ... **and make a 'shining shape' with our toes** ... lifting one foot at a time ... and opening the toes wide and moving them like they are twinkling ... with one foot ... and then the other ... and then let our feet make a firm base for our body. **Then, let's make a shining shape with our mouth** ... let it smile ... and share this smile with everyone in the group ..."

2 "**Now, let's feel our hands shining** ... turning our hands into a 'star' shape, with our fingers open wide ... and moving like twinkling stars ..."

3 "**Now, let's make our arms turn our whole body into a big star shape** ... open wide ... **and let's make our star shape bend** ... stretching up to the sky with one hand, while the other hand stretches down to the ground ... Then let's do

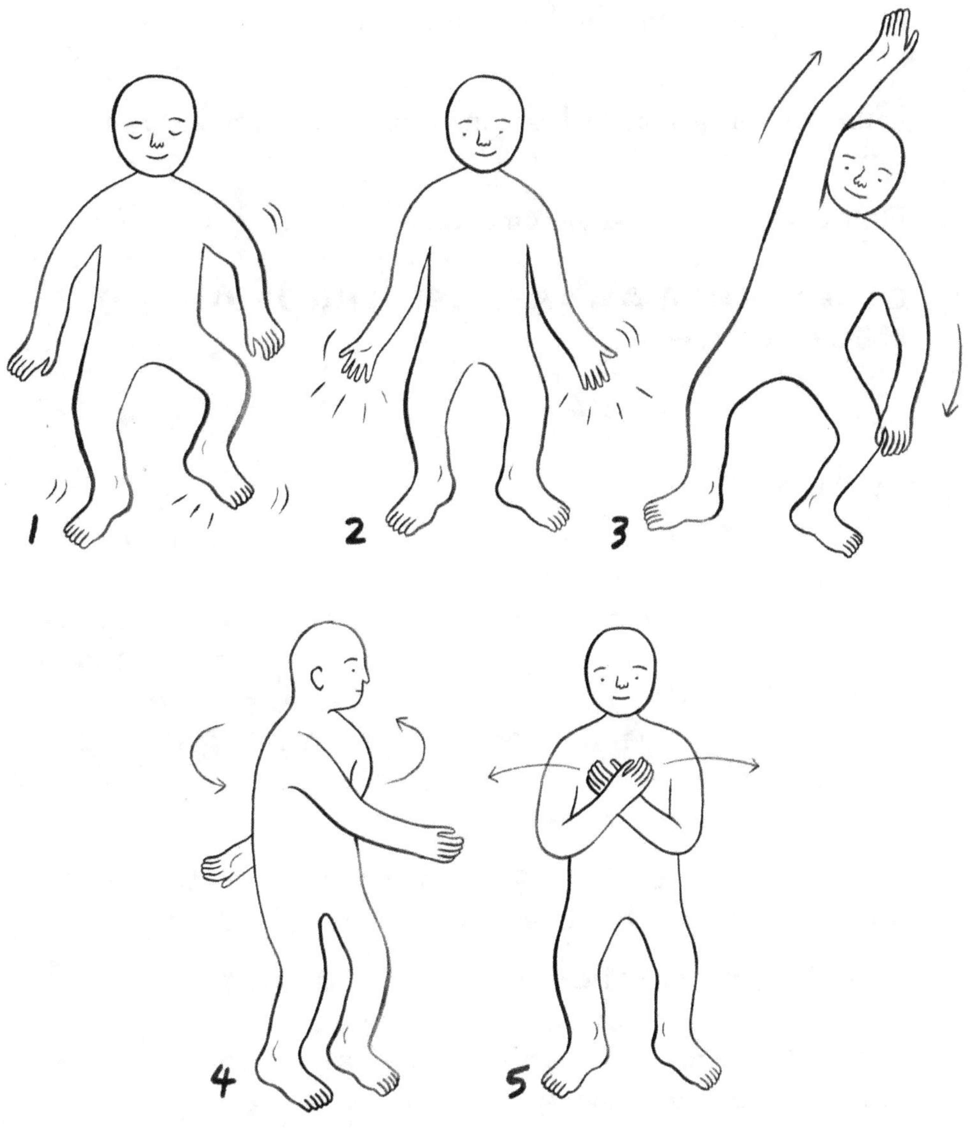

it to the other side ... The other hand stretching up to the sky, while the other hand stretches down to the ground ..."

4 "**Then let our 'star body' shine in circles** ... keeping our strong feet and legs still ... swinging our star hands and arms around the body ..."

5 "**Now, let's bring our hands to our heart** ... **and spread all the kindness out to share with everyone in the circle** ... breathing in, hands to the heart ... breathing out, hands shooting the kindness to everyone in the circle." (Repeat five times).

(Repeat sequence and finish with hands shooting kindness
to everyone).

Pause, with hands on the heart and tummy, and feel the breath
slowing down.

Flow to a quiet space to become still in a circle.

QUIET INNER AWARENESS/MINDFUL MEDITATION

Sitting practice

Stand in a circle.

"Take your place quietly in the circle ... and as you take a big, deep breath in, let your hands float up above your head ... to make the shape of a parachute ... breathing in, feel your body lift a little so you balance on your toes ... breathing out, feel your body sink a little, so your knees bend ... then feel your body softly, gently come to land in a sitting shape on the floor underneath your 'parachute arms' ... and let your arms float down beside you."

"Take it in turns to pass a smile to the person next to you, until the smile has travelled all the way around the group."

"**Now, lift your right hand above your head** ... (Teacher demonstrates) ... and let it softly come to rest over your heart. **Then bring your left hand to rest on the back of the person sitting next to you** (Teacher demonstrates) ..."

"**Let's close our eyes now**, so that we can shift from seeing ... to feeling with our bodies and hands. Beginning with noticing the breath ... and taking a big, deep breath in ... and feel it with the hand resting over the heart ... Then, **on the out-breath, let all the kindness from your hearts spread along the other arm to the back of the person next to you** ... spreading warm, caring feelings along our arms to the friend next to us ... Breathe into our heart to fill it up with calm, warm kindness ... and breathe out along our arm ... to share this kindness. Breathing the warm kindness into our heart ... and sharing it with the out-breath ... **Now we have created a circle of kindness**." (Pause to let children experience this in silence).

"**Now we can let our hands come to rest by gently holding hands with the friends sitting next to us**. Just sitting quietly, noticing the warm, soft touch of your hand holding another hand ... coming together in kindness ... and noticing your gentle, soft breath ... taking good care of you."

Children spend a few moments in stillness and silence to fully experience what they are feeling now.

"When you are ready ... take some slow, deep breaths ... and bring your attention back ... and do some big stretches through your arms and legs."

*Practice courtesy of Shakti Burke, 'Mindfulness in Education', Northern Rivers.

MINDFUL MOVEMENT / RITUAL 3

A 'Mindful Farewell' for the session

Invite everyone to return to a cross-legged sitting position.

"Bring your hands to press together (with palms facing in a 'prayer position') in a tight shape in front of your heart. Breathe in ... and as you slowly breathe out ... let your hands change into a soft shape, with all your fingers softening to create a soft space inside, just like the shape of a cocoon. Inside a cocoon, a butterfly is forming ... just like the beautiful changes inside us when we pause and make kind choices."

"**Hold your kind 'cocoon' hands in front of your heart**. Breathe in ... and as you breathe out, **bow in respect and kindness for yourself** ... Then, breathe in ... and breathe out ... and **bow with respect and kindness for others** ... Lastly, breathe in ... and breathe out, and **bow with respect and kindness for nature and the world**."

"Now, let your 'butterfly' hands open ... and smile ... sharing your beautiful smile with everyone ... and wave or twinkle all your fingers to spread your kindness to every person in the group."

Wonder and gratitude

TEACHER PREPARATION

RESOURCES

- Speaking Stick
- **Gifts from nature:** flowers, plants, herbs, fruit
- **Pictures:** nature scenes, families, pets
- Paper
- Coloured pencils/crayons
- **Music:** 'What a Wonderful World' by Louis Armstrong

LEARNING GOAL

To notice feeling glad and grateful

FOCUS WORDS

gladness
gratitude
appreciate and value

CHARACTER STRENGTHS

Zest (enthusiasm), gratitude, perspective (wisdom)

TIPS

Spend some time reflecting on what you would like to include in this session, to add meaning for the children. You might like to highlight or include learning from other sessions or refer to recent events or experiences that the children have had in the Centre or at home.

You could create a colourful 'Gratitude Board' for your room, featuring pictures, seasonal specimens from nature and children's drawings.

One of the benefits of practicing being Mindful is that it helps us to remember things. Simple things that we can easily forget – like pausing, calming down and remembering the things that really matter. Noticing what makes us truly happy and how fortunate we are.

Practising gratitude increases blood flow to key areas of the brain, causing a positive change in brain chemicals. This results in better sleep, greater alertness, enthusiasm, optimism and determination. Gratitude also builds social awareness and intelligence, deepening connections, and enhancing co-operation and collaboration with others.

DELIVERY OF SESSION

MINDFUL MOVEMENT / RITUAL 1

Music: 'What a Wonderful World' by Louis Armstrong.

Introduce a 'Mindful Pause', beginning the session with this practice.

"Stand in your space. Create a strong base with your feet and legs to hold your body … Let your back make a strong, straight shape … and let your head feel light … like it is a balloon floating on a string … Take a big, deep breath and let your hands float up to come together in a point above

your head. As you breathe out, let your hands slide down, and let one rest on your heart and the other on your tummy. Softly, quietly, say to yourself: 'Thank you body ... I will practise noticing what is kind for you now.' Then, let your hands give you a big hug."

Now flow to the practice below.

MINDFUL MOVEMENT / RITUAL 2

"Now, take another big, deep breath and let your hands float up to come together in a point above your head."

1 "As you breathe out, let your hands slide down, and pause in front of **your forehead**: breathe gently and notice **kind thoughts**."

2 "Take another big, deep breath ... and as you breathe out, let your hands slide down to pause in front of **your mouth**: breathe gently and notice **kind words**."

3 "Take another big, deep breath ... and as you breathe out, let your hands slide down to pause in front of **your heart**: breathe gently and notice **kind feelings** ... for yourself, others and the world."

Introduction for students

Share the following in your own words:

"Mindfulness helps us to remember what we are thinking, feeling and doing. A very important thing that we noticed in the last session is the need to remember to be kind."

"In this session, we will remember something else that is very important: feeling glad and grateful for all the good and beautiful things in life."

SHARING CIRCLE

Pass the Speaking Stick to a volunteer for each answer.

Q. What do you think the word 'gratitude' means?

A. We feel glad, thankful, pleased about something.

Q. Why do you think it is important to be grateful?

A. When we feel glad and grateful, we remember we are lucky, fortunate and blessed. This makes us feel happy.

Q. How can you show and tell people that you are grateful?

A. Smiling, nodding, saying 'thank you', 'I am pleased', 'I appreciate' – use words you think are appropriate.

Q. How does your body feel inside when you feel glad and grateful?

A. Invite responses from students – you might like to share with them how gratitude makes you feel.

ACTIVITY

Distribute sheets of paper, coloured pencils and crayons.

"Let's pause now to feel grateful that we have these beautiful coloured pencils/crayons, and grateful that we all have creative hands that can draw wonderful lines, shapes and patterns."

Listen to the words of Louis Armstrong in 'What a Wonderful World'.

Q. Why do you think the world is wonderful?

Q. What things would you like to draw on your sheet of paper to show what you are grateful to have in your life?" (Invite student to share ideas to stimulate creative thinking).

At the end of the activity, you might like to ask children to share with others what they drew, explaining their choice of colours and shapes.

MINDFUL MOVEMENT

Qigong – 'Splash Water, Paint the Rainbow'

Music: 'What a Wonderful World' by Louis Armstrong.

1 "**Stand with your feet comfortably spaced … and knees slightly bent** … as if you are sitting on a horse! Notice the shape you are in … feeling your back strong and straight … chest open … shoulders soft … and head floating like a balloon over your body."

"Feel your arms hanging soft and loose beside your body … palms facing forward …"

2 "**Breathing in … let your arms float up to just over your head** … like you are splashing clear, sparkling water over your body … and on the out-breath, let them float back down." (Repeat five times).

"**Now let's make a different shape** with different moves … Breathing in … **let your arms float above your head** … and breathing out …"

3 "**Let your hands and arms draw a half circle over your head, just like a rainbow … Pause in line with your**

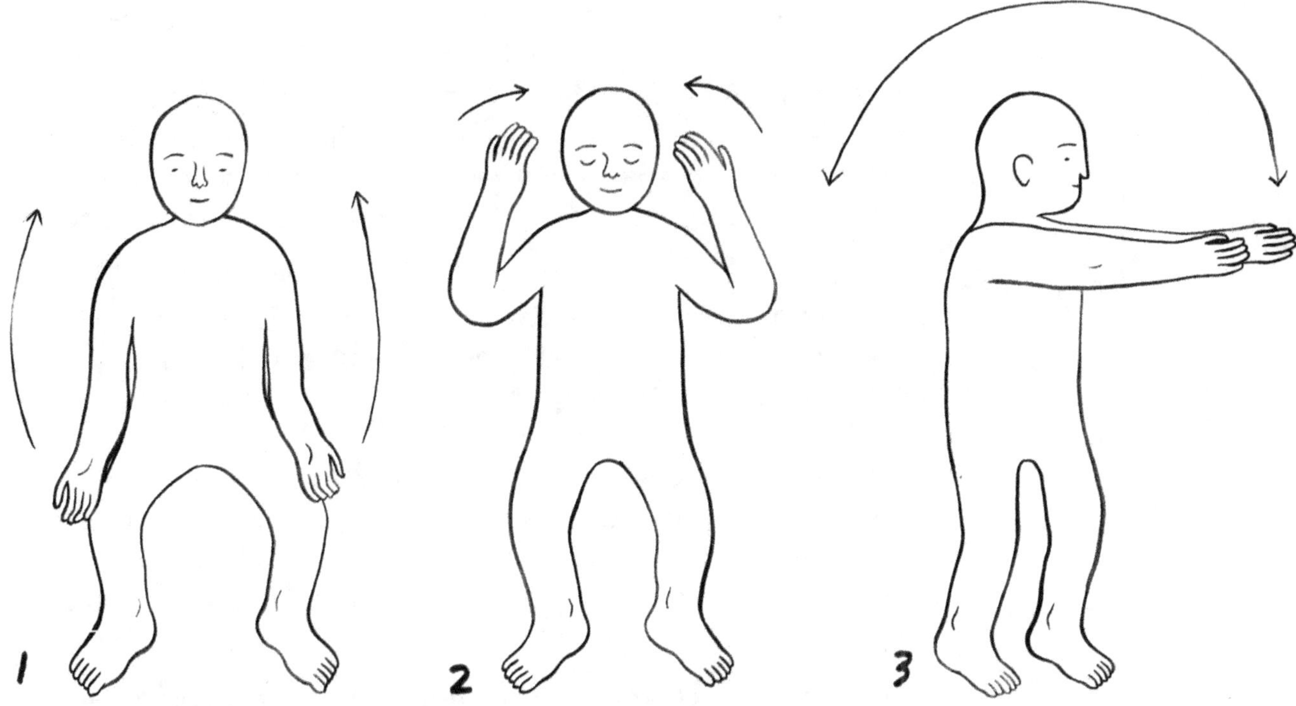

shoulders ... Breathing in, let them imagine painting a beautiful rainbow over the body ... hands floating back above the head ... and breathing out, hands floating back to the other side ... finish 'painting the rainbow' over to the other side." (Repeat five times).

Now flow to the practice below.

QUIET INNER AWARENESS/MINDFUL MEDITATION

Sitting and lying down practice

"Take up your position in your quiet space ... letting your body return to standing still ..."

"**Let's pause to feel grateful for everyone in the group now** ... Remembering all the kind things they do ... and all the things that you value and like about them ... Say a quiet 'thank you' ... by sharing a smile with everyone."

"Let's pause now **to feel gratitude for your feet** ... looking down at them ... and feeling glad that they work so well ... Grateful that they hold you up all day ... and feeling grateful for all the things they can do: working with your strong legs

... to walk, run, jump, skip, hop, dance, climb ... Now they can be grateful to you, for letting them have a rest ... for letting them be still ... So now, take all your weight off your wonderful feet ... and let them find their resting place on the floor with your legs ... Let your **whole body** feel grateful and happy as you come down to find a safe, calm resting space to sit on the floor ..."

"**Let's notice our eyes now** ... feeling grateful and glad that they work so well ... Looking and seeing clearly ... all day. Your eyes might be very grateful to rest now ... so notice your eyelids gratefully, softly, closing down ... to rest over your eyes ... **And when your eyes rest**, so can your head ... **And so can your brain** ... There is nothing your brain has to do, or think about now ... **Noticing all the parts of your body** gratefully slowing down to be calm and still ... and letting your whole body lie down on the floor ..."

"**Feeling your clever, capable hands now** ... and pause, feeling glad for all the things your hands do for you: making things; helping you eat, wash, get dressed; opening and closing things; catching, playing and climbing ... Remembering all the kind things your hands can do ... **Now your hands and arms can be grateful to you** ... for choosing to let them be quiet and still ... soft and calm ... resting beside you."

"**Feeling grateful for your whole body** ... all the muscles and bones... and your heart and tummy and all the organs and cells that take care of you all day ... and every day. **Now you are taking care of them** ... just letting them deeply rest for a while ... **Feeling grateful for the breath** ... as it just breathes you ... softly and gently ... flowing in and out ... back and forth."

Children spend a few moments in stillness and silence to fully experience what they are feeling now.

"When you are ready ... take some slow, deep breaths ... Bring your attention back ... and enjoy some big stretches through your arms and legs."

A 'Mindful Farewell' for the session

Invite everyone to return to a cross-legged sitting position.

"Bring your hands to press together (with palms facing in a 'prayer position') in a tight shape in front of your heart. Breathe in … and as you slowly breathe out … let your hands change into a soft shape, with all your fingers softening to create a soft space inside, just like the shape of a cocoon. Inside a cocoon, a butterfly is forming … just like the beautiful changes inside us when we pause and make kind choices."

"**Hold your kind 'cocoon' hands in front of your heart**. Breathe in … and as you breathe out, **bow in respect and kindness for yourself** … Then, breathe in … and breathe out … and **bow with respect and kindness for others** … Lastly, breathe in … and breathe out, and **bow with respect and kindness for nature and the world**."

"Now, let your 'butterfly' hands open … and smile … sharing your beautiful smile with everyone … and wave or twinkle all your fingers to spread your kindness to every person in the group."

SESSION 12
Discovering peace

TEACHER PREPARATION

RESOURCES

- Speaking Stick
- **The Mindful Gift Box:** a colourful gift box
- Different coloured ribbons
- **Glass jewels:** small, coloured glass beads
- Battery candle/light
- **Music:** 'La Petite Fille De La Mer' by Vangelis for Mindful Rituals and Movement and 'This Little Light of Mine', Bible Songs for Children for Activity

FOCUS WORDS

gift
goodness
centre
peace

CHARACTER STRENGTHS

Love, kindness, gratitude

LEARNING GOAL

To notice when and how we can feel peaceful

TIPS

Reflect on what peace means to you. When do you notice feeling peaceful? How can you bring about a state of peace?

Mindfulness practices enable the 'golden gift' of experiencing peaceful moments. This can be a very important discovery for children to make.

Often it can seem as though the ability to feel peaceful is far away. A sense that we can only feel peaceful when certain conditions apply – the right weather, place, conditions or time.

This session helps children discover that peace exists inside the self and we can practice being connected to this quiet centre, *remembering that deep within every person lies an inner goodness.*

DELIVERY OF SESSION

MINDFUL MOVEMENT / RITUAL 1

Music: 'La Petite Fille De La Mer' by Vangelis.

Introduce a 'Mindful Pause', beginning the session with this practice.

"Stand in your space. Create a strong base with your feet and legs to hold your body … Let your back make a strong, straight shape … and let your head feel light … like it is a balloon floating on a string … Take a big, deep breath and let your hands float up to come together in a point above your head. As you breathe out, let your hands slide down, and let one rest on your heart and the other on your tummy. Softly, quietly, say to yourself: 'Thank you body … I will practise noticing what is kind for you now.' Then, let your hands give you a big hug."

Now flow to the practice below.

MINDFUL MOVEMENT / RITUAL 2

"Now, take another big, deep breath and let your hands float up to come together in a point above your head."

1 "As you breathe out, let your hands slide down, and pause in front of **your forehead**: breathe gently and notice **kind thoughts**."

2 "Take another big, deep breath … and as you breathe out, let your hands slide down to pause in front of **your mouth**: breathe gently and notice **kind words**."

3 "Take another big, deep breath … and as you breathe out, let your hands slide down to pause in front of **your heart**: breathe gently and notice **kind feelings** … for yourself, others and the world."

Share the following in your own words:

"In the past two sessions we have noticed what is kind and what it feels like to be glad and grateful."

"A wonderful thing to notice is when we feel peaceful. In this session, we will notice how peace is a state that silently waits inside our bodies for us to discover that it is there."

SHARING CIRCLE

Pass the Speaking Stick to a volunteer for each answer.

Q. What do you think the word 'peace' means?

A. Words could include freedom, contentment, quiet, ease, stillness and silence.

Q. When do you notice that you are feeling peaceful?

A. Invite responses. However, if children do not respond, offer an example of when you notice you are at peace, before moving to the next question.

Q. Is there a special time and place when you notice you are feeling peaceful?

A. Remind children of simple, everyday experiences, such as lying on the grass under a tree, in the bath, in bed, hugging Mum and Dad and cuddling a pet.

Q. Do you think feeling peaceful is possible wherever you are?

A. (Invite responses ... and then lead to 'Introduction to Activity').

Share the following in your own words:

"We are going to notice that peaceful feelings are never far away. We can learn how to remember to calm down and connect to these quiet, gentle feelings. Peaceful states are always waiting deep inside our body, just waiting for us to notice them!"

ACTIVITY

Place the gift box in the centre of the space and invite children to sit in a circle around it. Remind children that every person has gifts and the greatest gift of all is the goodness inside. (Remind them of the song 'This Little Light of Mine' – you might like to play it gently in the background).

Slowly peel away the different coloured ribbons. Ask children what feelings they think each colour could be.

Show children that at the very bottom there is a light: "Sometimes when we feel sad or worried, we forget this peaceful light, but it is always there, waiting for us to notice it. Next to the light, there are little 'gems' that reflect the light, just like our Mindful Pauses that let light into our lives."

"In this little 'Gift Box' the light and gems are deep inside. We cannot see them when the lid is on and they are covered over with lots of feelings." (The ribbons).

"It is the same for us. When we are full of busy feelings, we forget about our special, calm centre. However, it is always quietly, patiently, waiting to share light, warmth and peace with us!"

(As you are talking, slowly peel away one ribbon after another to reveal the light and gems lying at the bottom).

MINDFUL MOVEMENT

Create your own 'Mindful Bubble'

Music: 'La Petite Fille De La Mer' by Vangelis.

1 "**Stand with your feet comfortably spaced ... and knees slightly bent** ... as if you are sitting on a horse! Notice the shape you are in ... feeling your back strong and straight ... chest open ... shoulders soft ... and head floating like a balloon over your body."

"We are going to create a very 'special space' now, with our arms and hands ... To help you feel the shape, and see it in your mind, it is good to let your eyes close."

2 "**Feel yourself taking in a big ... slow ... deep breath** in ... and as it flows in, **let your hands feel light as a feather ... floating upwards with the in-breath ... making this**

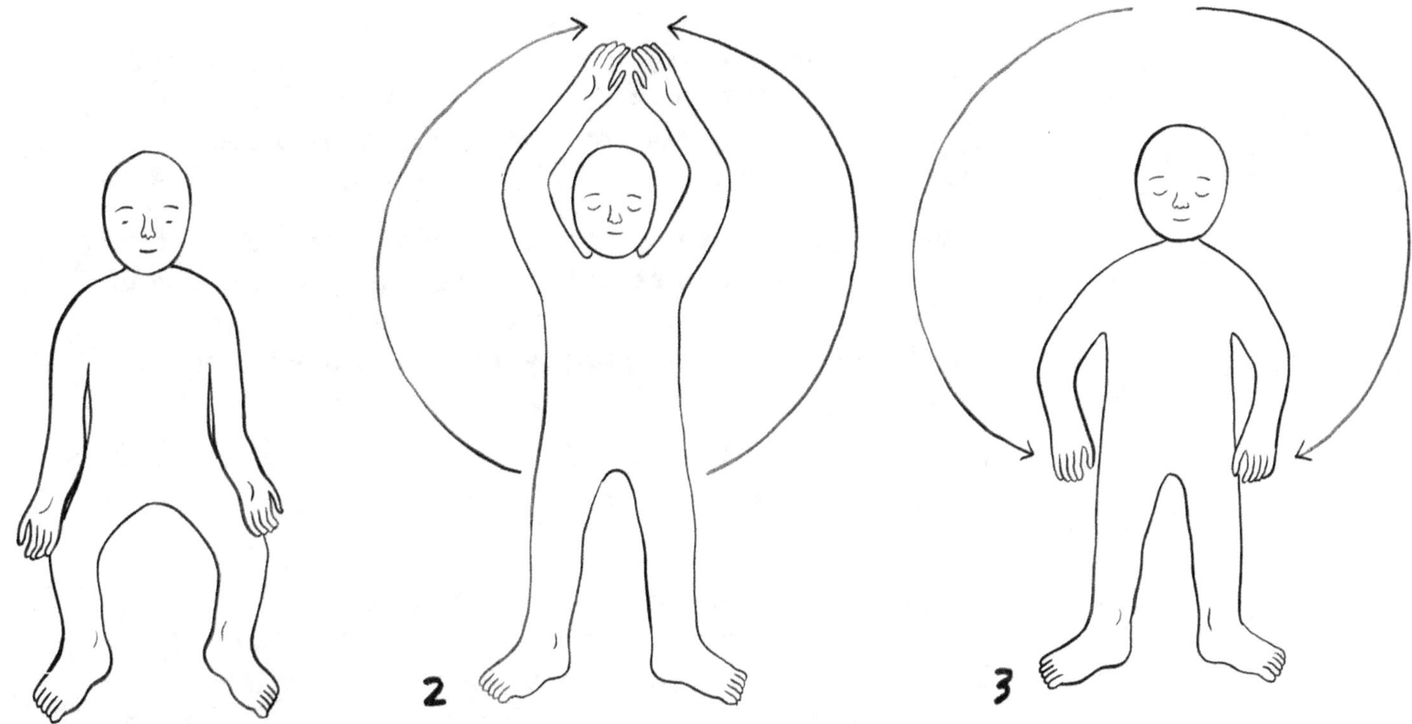

beautiful round shape, like a shiny, clear bubble all around you … Feel your fingers silently, gently touch above your head …"

3 "As you breathe out … **let your hands float back down** … **You might like to imagine that all your fingers are little paint brushes** … and as they move, **they are painting your beautiful 'Mindful Bubble' all around you** … What colour is your bubble? … Every time you breathe in … and out … let your bubble become more and more beautiful … Softly … gently … silently … making your very own Mindful Space … feeling your body inside your bubble … Feeling happy, calm and peaceful." (Repeat 5 times).

Flow to …

QUIET INNER AWARENESS/MINDFUL MEDITATION

Lying down practice

"Notice your body moving down into its special shape, to be still and quiet. For this practice, **your body can choose a lying down shape**."

"Letting your body find its quiet place … and space … on the floor. **Let's begin with your eyes** … They can have a special treat and rest from all that looking and seeing … by gently closing down. **Allow your feet and legs return to being quiet and still …"**

"**Now it is your hands and arms turn to be soft** … quiet and still. **Let the gift of quiet and calm feelings spread into your body … through your bottom and hips … along your back … into your chest and through your heart … flowing all the way through your shoulders, neck … and head.**"

(Begin quietly walking around the group, and one by one, place a glass gem/bead in between the eyebrows of each child).

"**Just let your head find a lovely still space to be** … So still, that when I place the little gem in the space between your eyebrows, it will stay there. **Notice what the gem feels like** … Does it feel cool … big or small… smooth or rough? … Does it feel heavy or light?"

"**This little gem helps you notice the space between your eyebrows** … and every time you breathe in, you can imagine a peaceful space … like a gentle light, softly glowing … and when you breathe out … this gentle light can spread all through your face … and down into your body …" (Pause to allow time for children to fully experience).

"**This little gem can remind you that you will always have a safe, calm, peaceful space deep inside** … When you become very quiet and still, you can notice it … and every time you notice it, calm, peaceful feelings can grow inside you."

Children spend a few moments in stillness and silence to fully experience what they are feeling now.

"When you are ready … take some slow, deep breaths. Bring your attention back … and have some big stretches through your arms and legs."

(Collect the gems and place back in the box, to be used when the practice is repeated).

A 'Mindful Farewell' for the session

Invite everyone to return to a cross-legged sitting position.

"Bring your hands to press together (with palms facing in a 'prayer position') in a tight shape in front of your heart. Breathe in ... and as you slowly breathe out ... let your hands change into a soft shape, with all your fingers softening to create a soft space inside, just like the shape of a cocoon. Inside a cocoon, a butterfly is forming ... just like the beautiful changes inside us when we pause and make kind choices."

"**Hold your kind 'cocoon' hands in front of your heart**. Breathe in ... and as you breathe out, **bow in respect and kindness for yourself** ... Then, breathe in ... and breathe out ... and **bow with respect and kindness for others** ... Lastly, breathe in ... and breathe out, and **bow with respect and kindness for nature and the world**."

"Now, let your 'butterfly' hands open ... and smile ... sharing your beautiful smile with everyone ... and wave or twinkle all your fingers to spread your kindness to every person in the group."

Sustaining and growing Mindfulness

"Attention is the most basic form of love. By paying attention we let ourselves be touched by life and our hearts naturally become more open and engaged."
— TARA BRACH

Touched by life: the heart and mind are inextricably connected. A state of presence unites all parts of the body, mind and brain, with satisfying connections to our inner and outer worlds. Kind awareness unites us, keeping us in touch and nurturing precious relationships.

When we practise noticing, we are practising developing the quality of our attention – where it is and what we are thinking, feeling and doing.

In writing this book, my intention has been to provide you and your children with a rich, creative Mindfulness framework.

It is my wish that this book will be a catalyst for you to embed Mindfulness in your Centre, therapeutic practice or home – and ultimately, to go beyond the constructs of the program. I hope that you develop a sense of confidence and competence as Mindfulness guides, connecting children with their unique inner gifts and creative possibilities.

Staff at the' 'ELC One' Centre in Cranbourne who trialled this program decided to spend extra time working through the sessions. The pace at which you proceed with your children is entirely up to you. It is a program that could be used over 12 weeks, six months or a year.

A Mindfulness foundation can be built on every day, developing the precious skills of awareness and kind choices.

You can use short, simple practices to provide 'Mindful Punctuation' to bookend the day, for greetings and farewells, ways to refresh focus, support transitions and introduce new activities.

Longer Mindful Meditations work at a deeper level, enabling children to develop an intimate, friendly connection with their inner world while gently rewiring the brain to enhance focus and concentration.

In the enlightened words of Eleanor Roosevelt, "The purpose of life is to live it, to taste experience to the utmost, to reach out eagerly and without fear for newer and richer experience."

Review the rich 'Mindful Palette' of possibilities:

- Pausing Practices to connect to senses in the now: sight, sound, taste, smell, touch/feel, balance, movement
- Mindful Movements, combined with 'Ritual Greeting and Farewell' practices.
- Breath awareness
- Awareness of choices
- Awareness of Character Strengths
- Developing and organising your class resources.

HERE ARE MORE SUGGESTIONS FOR YOU

Connect to nature

Nature is our fundamental source of wellbeing. In the busyness of life, living in large cities with rampant development, connection to nature is becoming scarce for most of us. Numerous studies attest to the health benefits from spending time in nature.

It is wonderful for children to care for plants and animals and focus the beam of kindness to all living things!

Simple ways to create nature connections:

- Lying on the grass and gazing at clouds.
- Digging a hole in soil and discovering what lies beneath the surface.
- Walking Meditation, with bare feet on the grass. Create a sensory walking Meditation path! Plant simple, hardy herbs along it

(rosemary, lavender, mint etc) and alternate patches of sand, grass
and smooth river pebbles. In hot weather moisten with water.
• Treasure Hunts: to find different seeds, bugs, flowers, leaves,
  bark and feathers.
• Make 'nature rubbings' with crayons and paper (rub over leaves,
  bark, gravel, rocks) and use them for collage, murals or to make
  paper chains to remember that everything in life is connected.

A gratitude board

Invite children to pin reminders of blessings in life: dried flowers/
herbs, drawings, cards, pictures etc. Keep adding and changing
the content.

A seasonal table

Follow the Steiner tradition and set up a table to display the
highlights of each season. For impact you could use a different
coloured table cloth for each season, with special fabrics or
symbols for celebrations that you would like to observe, such as
Christmas, Hanukkah, Ramadan, International Peace Day etc.

Mindful mobiles

Over the years I have had the privilege of working with heartful,
creative and inspirational educators. It has been a thrill to see
their kind, Mindful teaching practices and creations. These have
included beautiful, simple Mindful mobiles, featuring children's
drawings of faces and bodies in favourite poses and shapes and
specimens from nature. One teacher dragged a beautiful branch
that she found on the way to school to create a Mindful mobile
suspended over children's desks.

Mindful spaces

Some schools have taken the exceptional step of creating a
Mindfulness Room. Dedicated teachers in one primary school
claimed an old portable classroom, and with the help of students,
cleaned it out and kitted it out to become a wondrous space,
adorned with a Meditation quilt, cushions and all kinds of props.
Other classroom teachers have created little havens, in corners
of the room. Children have painted murals and netting, lights,
cushions and even beach umbrellas have created magical havens for
children to enjoy moments of respite and quiet.

Singing and moving together fire mirror neurons and synchronise bodies, minds and hearts in joyful ways.

There are all kinds of ways to use mirroring practices. I saw a video clip of an elementary school in America where the day starts with children facing each other in pairs, mirroring hand movements and singing 'Twinkle, twinkle little star … what a beautiful child you are!" What a wonderful way to start the day.

Simple songs, that children know and love, can be adapted. It is great for the children to create their own lyrics, creating another opportunity for them to grow agency with the practices.

I use 'The Hokey Pokey' song for this purpose. We create a circle, and I start with the words: "Put your Mindless Self OUT (and we all make a crazy shape) … and your Mindful Self IN (we make a calm shape) … Your Mindless Self Out, we do the Mindful Shuffle and we turn around … That's what it's all about! Oh, the Mindful Shuffle, Oh, the Mindful Shuffle … That's what it's all about!

Then let the children take turns to contribute different words and movements.

Simple songs and movements bring wonderful ways to enhance learning. Children who are attuned kinaesthetically really benefit from these practices. Stepping the feet and moving hands with the rhythm of music create ways for children to learn left from right, front and back, the directions of north, south, east and west and the numbers on a clock.

Anything that we achieve in life requires consistent commitment. Growing a kind, capable, creative mind is one of life's greatest achievements. Practising Mindfulness helps to make the most of the mind: moment by moment, day by day.

Enjoy every moment with the children in your care as they create a curious, kind, creative head-heart start for their lives.